The

Amusings

of

JEREMY FINE

by Barry Brent

Revelation Press
Toronto

Published by:
Revelation Press,
Box 27089
500 Rexdale Blvd.
Etobicoke, Ontario
M9W 6L0

Printed and bound in Canada
Cover design by Barry Brent and David Sztybel.
Cover graphic and typesetting by David Sztybel.

First Printing September 1994
Second Printing November 1994
Third Printing April 1995

Distributed by
Cannon Book Distribution Ltd.
1 800 216-2985

Canadian Cataloguing in Publication Data

Brent, Barry
     The amusings of Jeremy Fine

Poems.
ISBN 0-9698590-0-7

I. Title.

PS8553.R45A78 1994   C811'.54   C94-931972-4
PR9199.3.B74A78 1994

The Cast
(in order of appearance)

Jeremy
Mom
Dad
Grandpa
Uncle Sid
Cousin Phil
Cousin Rhonda
Brother Ted
Jill, Ted's girlfriend
Mule, a drummer
Sister Sue
Cousin Steve
A Neighbor
Uncle Lee
Aunt Vi
Cousin Cliff
Aunt Nana
Uncle Sam
Aunt Sherri
Uncle Delbert
Aunt Claire
Aunt Lil

ACTUAL PAGES . . . SPANNING THE AGES

You hold here an interactive (you can write in it), user-friendly (you can carry it in your purse or pocket), recyclable (but not right away, hopefully), post-modern (always in advance of any other technology) artifact — a BOOK.

Never obsolete . . . never out of fashion.

A rock in a sea of change.

'Tis pleasant, sure, to see one's name in print,
A book's a book, although there's nothing in't.

—Byron, *E.B. and S.R.*

. . . a few cubicles away [was] a mild, ineffectual,
dreamy creature named Ampleforth, with very
hairy ears and a surprising talent for juggling
rhymes and meters . . .

—Orwell, *1984*

These are the rhymes that try men's souls.

—Anon.

This is a work of fiction.
The views expressed by
the characters are entirely
 their own.

It is not a collection,
but rather an integrated opus.

DEDICATION

In loving memory

of my

Mother and Father

THIS BOOK IS ALSO DEDICATED . . .

. . . to you, dear reader,
    however you got it,
but especially
    if you went and bought it.

1

I used to ride a tricycle
but now I have a bicycle,
    and in the shed
    a real cool sled—
I've labelled it The Icycle.

2

But what I'd really
    really like
is roaring on
    a motorbike.

When others speed
    you'll see me matching,
varoomatism
    is so catching.

3

At school I've tools to write with,
and classmates to recite with;
    and best of all,
    out in the hall,
a lot of friends to fight with.

4

Ancient History

We have a cafeteria
whose food is not superia;
    it's often cold
    and so darn old
it dates back to Assyria.

5

The fast lane

I have to do everything on the run—
get washed,
get dressed,
eat a bun;
make my lunch too—
Whew!
By the time I'm finished I'm hardly done.

6

Playing it cool

I'd a hole in my sock—
it started to talk,
    saying "Darn it!"

So you know what I did?
I lifted the lid
of our laundry bin
and stuffed it right in.
    That'll larn it!

Next I tripped on a chair
that should not have been *there*;
    but I, in good grace,
    just examined my face
and made the repair
(to my face, not the chair).

Then my bike got a flat—
at first I just sat;
    then, wise to its tricks,
I trundled it home
    for my Dad to fix.

I might seem at first blush
   a bit unkind,
   but why
   should I
let anything smush
   my peace of mind?

7

Count your missings

I don't got a dog and I don't got a cat,
I don't got this and I don't got that;
you could fill a library, every spot,
with all the things that I don't got.

But two skinned elbows and two skinned knees,
suppertime goodies like carrots and peas,
hassles from parents and brotherly punches—
those kinds of things I got in bunches.

8

Seen it all

Did you ever run
   as fast as fast,
and still come in
   the very last?
I've done that often,
   but no more;
now I even walk
   to the candy store.

9

I love popping popcorn in the popcorn popper,
every little grain becomes a great big whopper;
they look so entertaining as they ricochet
       and sputter,
and they're looking even better when they're
       drowned in melted butter.

10

Birthday Blues

A party they gave my friend Steven
I would have been better off leavin';
    'cause all that I snarfed up
    I later on barfed up,
which means that I just came out even.

11

For doctors I've really no use;
I go, but I want to vamoose;
    my Mom says I shocked her
    by saying the doctor
I only feel good with is Seuss.

12

Dentists, too,
    are on my list
of folks I'm able
    to resist.
But Mom's a stickler
    for each session:
"Your teeth should make
    a good impression."

4

13

In summer I love
    camping out,
(though poison ivy
    casts a doubt).

But you'll never ever
    live as well—
you sleep in a Billion-
    Star hotel.

14

My Grandpa said
    as we walked downtown,
"I'm slowing up
    and I'm slowing down."

I thought that odd
    and I told him so;
"They're both the same",
    he explained, "although

If you asked me why
    I couldn't say—
which probably proves
    the point, in a way."

15

The Team

Some day we're going to be grown up,
some day we're going to win the Cup;
some day the TV news will name us,
some day we'll all be rich and famous;
and now we're going outside to play,
and practice for that great Some Day.

16

Whenever I'm finding life a bore
I drop into a humor store;
today the guy said, "Sorry, jock,
we're cleaned right out of laughing stock."

17

It really gets me when they say
"Give me a break" or "Make my day";
they'll do them both if they'll refrain
from using either one again.
You'll never hear clichés from me,
they're simply not my cup of tea.

18

A bad day

My best friend gets mad
    and calls me a phony;
I open my lunch—
    it's macaroni;
hightailing homeward
    I drop my Sony;
I go to the fridge—
    we're out of spumoni!
That's it. Game over.
    Bring on the Zamboni.

19

A true best friend is hard to find,
"There's plenty of the other kind."
I thought I'd found the one in Freddie,
but, like the rest, he proved unsteady.
It's not that I insist they do much,
but always be there: is that too much?
Friendship with me is not a whim,
I almost always stood by *him*.

20

We look for friends
    to share things with,
but friendship's mostly
    hit and myth.

21

Oh would some Power
    the giftie gie me
to make them see me
    as *I* see me.

22

We're each unique,
    the one and only,
and therefore not
    uniquely lonely.

23

Be tolerant like me

I can't stand people
    who condemn
other people
    just like them.

24

One thing about being a kid
    is wild—
you're in touch with your outer
    and inner child.

But I'm not so sure,
    despite what they natter,
I'd be really that thrilled
    to hang on to the latter.

25

Exams are coming so I cram;
who said "I think, therefore I am"?
It makes me feel—this hurts a lot—
I cannot think, therefore I'm not.

26

I'm cramming *Macbeth*,
    I'm tearing my hair,
I'm one step away
    from intensive care.

"Lay off, Macduff",
    my brain's transmitting,
"that ravelled sleave
    needs major knitting."

27

Zanzibar's easy, but . . .

Zimbabwe, Zambia,
    Zaire,
often get confused,
    I fear.
How they're
    differentiated
marks the truly
    zeducated.

28

The throw ups

"Wake up", "Grow up",
    "Smarten up" too;
a lot of "ups"
    get thrown at you.

They're not said smiling,
    but with a frown;
these are the ups
    that put you down.

29

The dreamer's revenge

I'm going to be an astronaut
and stay in space an awful lot,
and then I'll laugh for all I'm worth
at folks who say "Get down to earth."

30

They don't teach grammar
    anymore,
'cause most agree
    it would be a bore.

But it leads to lots
    of writing anguish:
what we're talking 'bout here
    is English languish.

31

Computers

If you're going to write
    you have to have one—
check it out
    with the Bard of Avon.

32

I'll never make a hero
of Roman ruler Nero;
    with Rome in roons
    he fiddled tunes—
I call him Nero Zero.

33

The early Christians had their share
    of grief: the Emperor despised them;
though *he* might counter, "Au contraire:
    we lionized them."

34

I came, I saw, I went haywire

A vastly overrated geezer
(it seems to me) is Julius Caesar;
to start with, someone must be bonkers
who comes, sees—then goes out and conquers.
I guess his name is just a teaser
that begs for altered spelling: "Seizer."

35

Caesar the Soldier
    conquered Gaul,
but Caesar the Salad
    conquers all.

If this reflection
    has a moral,
it's just that lettuce
    bears the laurel.

36

Et tu, Freddie?

Although they're kind of bloody,
    those Roman stories suit us;
reminds us, as we study,
    there's lots of friends like Brutus.

37

Not so great

The thing with Alexander,
he wanted to be grander;
    the slightest slight
    when he was tight
and up would go his dander.

You're not a fuddy-duddy
to think it's kind of cruddy
    to grab a spear
    and drive it clear
through your old bosom buddy.

38

These heroes had
    a goodly run,
and now it's on
    to other fun.

The future points
    an opposite path,
where homage shuns
    the greats of wrath.

39

Excuse a commercial
    innuendo,
but would these guys have warred
    if they'd had Nintendo?

40

We know that Peace
    is Earth's first need;
soldiers are
    a dying breed.

41

I'd feel a bit odd
    in a uniform—still,
I have to admit
    I'd be dressed to kill.

42

Henry the Eighth liked to see people crawlin'—
a two-door mini edition of Stalin.
To further belittle the women he wed
he gleefully shortened them by a head.

43

Hello Columbus

We've studied the conquistadors,
those highly honored conquerors;
how, with a few, they vanquished millions,
and sent home treasure by the billions.

The native peoples were employed
in mines and fields, and then destroyed;
no matter that they gave their trust,
they lost their gold, then bit the dust.

And South America today
seems just to pay, and pay, and pay;
pollution, murdered kids, drug wars,
the gift of the conquistadors.

44

Two ten-year-olds
    killed a child of two;
this hideous crime
    grabbed world-wide view.

Brazil's where killing
    of children's at,
but adults do it
    so that's old hat.

45

The Inquisition

The reign
in Spain
was quite insane,
and fell mainly
on the plain
and humble.

It was called "religion",
but saw every smidgen
of basic humanity
crumble.

Gray-haired women
burned alive
so Satan's patriarchy
might thrive.

46

Autos-da-fé

Fear-ridden crowds
    shouted olé!
as black-robed fryers
    staged their play.

"Acts of faith"
    they called these games,
where they shot humanity
    down in flames.

47

Ages ago
    the verdict was in:
a burning faith
    is a cardinal sin.

48

They called it "love"
    (as still they do);
which proves that Newspeak's
    hardly new.

49

The gods of irony
    supply us
names like Innocent
    and Pius.

Giving the devil his due

The Jesuits fine-tuned
    racial hate,
based on blood
    in divisions of eight.

They honed the art
    of inflicting pain
to a point that was never
    quite reached again.

(Though their deeds were studied
    by Hitler and Himmler,
who did their damnedest
    to do something sim'lar.)

If we're giving out grades,
    check the Jesuits' bid;
they were clearly the best
    at what they did.

They had various ways
    to spread their joy,
but cutting out tongues
    was a common ploy.

It wasn't severe
    like the rack or wheel,
just a Jesuit warning,
    no big deal.

Lambs for the slaughter

New continents beckon!
    Hell's legions form up!
The doings in Europe
    were just a warm-up.

Apocalypse

Ninety million
    souls alive—
four decades later,
    down to five.

If medals were
    awarded for
murder by
    the million-score,

Challenges
    would quickly fold—
they've no competitors
    for gold.

54

What goes around . . .

History's greatest
    murderthon—
for gold: how soon
    the gold was gone!

Strewn on heedless
    ocean floors,
expended on
    forgotten wars—

One day a ship
    sailed out from Spain[*]
with every last
    accursèd grain.

55

In Newfoundland
    the Beothuk
ran into settlers
    and out of luck.

A papal nod,
    a priestly wink,
they soon became
    a missing link.

---

[*]from Cartagena to Odessa, October 1936.

Holy Smoke

Apologies? Rather
    in curia praise;
they carry a torch
    for the good old days.

Those are the days
    they cherish most,
when people who stood in their way
    were toast.

Horsemen of the Apocalypse

No apology?
    Prudent, then,
to assume they're hot
    to trot again.

James Joyce plunged
    his rapier home
when he punned that "There's
    no plagues like Rome."

59

Let us prey

Father Tiso's slaughter
 of Czech and Slovak—
the Vatican death camp
 at Jasenovac—

That old "Holy Office"
 is still working well,
creating on Earth
 its monster-god's hell.

60

Hate your neighbor

The blood libel spewed
 by the Vatican State
powered a rising
 tide of hate

To a landmark Vatican
 victory:
six million swept
 by the Holy See.

61

Napoleon smashed
 the ghetto wall,
and papal might
 was in free-fall—

But the Vatican
 trumped its belittler
with its own white knight on horseback—
 Hitler.

666

Here's something new
    beneath the sun:
6 million plus
    the pius one.

When 666
    gave up the ghost,
the stench drove medics
    from their post.

Putrescent flesh—
    we won't go near it,
but few detect
    putrescent spirit.

It's not unnatural,
    what they do—
the cowbird does it,
    the cuckoo too.

The hatched usurper
    is unfulfilled
until the legitimate
    offspring's killed.

65

The Holocaust,
    their most treasured stat,
has boomeranged
    on the blood-brimmed Vat:

Racism, the weapon
    they forged and used,
has been discredited,
    dulled, defused.

66

Trying to cover
    the spoor of its crime,
the Vatican has
    the devil's own time.

67

They're sure they have
    sufficient clout
to turn the record
    inside-out.

Not in our lifetime,
    but their view
is long: they know
    what time can do.

For now, enough
    to nudge the rap in:
did it really,
    truly happen?

(Always keeping
    well concealed
their sponsorship
    of this new field.)

Eventually,
    truth demised,
the Holocaust
    Columbusized.

68

Midland, Ontario

"Cet animal
    est très méchant—
quand on l'attaque
    il se défend."

As soon as Natives
    crossed the line,
we up and got
    a Martyrs' Shrine.

69

Murder will out

Though they rewrite the past
    in order to suit your
sane human instincts,
    that past has no future.

70

Their long-range plan's
    clear as a bell—
destroy the State
    of Israel.

While it exists,
    the Holocaust
stands not a chance
    of getting lost.

And that forebodes
    the kind of fate
their bladders void
    to contemplate.

They mangle history
    with their lies,
but *being* history—
    quelle surprise.

71

How can such evil
    dupe the world's thinkers?
The wages of sin
    buy lots of blinkers.

And who wants to see
    the leering phony
behind the mask
    of sanctimony?

Truth has been forced
    to close up shop
in the face of Vatican
    agitprop.

72

Pope dope

Hamlet found it
  revelatory
that the lips can smile
  while the hands are gory.

73

In the unending war
  between good and evil,
our sense of who's who
  needs a real upheaval.

74

The papacy Macbethed

When all the ghastly crimes
are open to the view
of all, layer upon layer,
  world without end of grief,
then will he feel *his title*
hang loose about him, like
a giant's robe upon
  a dwarfish thief.

75

Who ever dreamed
    the papacy
could still encumber
    Italy?

Once, Roman freemen
    showed their fiber
by pitching pontiffs
    in the Tiber.

76

Veritatis Splendor

Pap's the norm
    anent the pope,
but bitter truth's
    our only hope.

77

It's important to call
    a spade a spade,
'cause that's the thing
    that can dig your grave.

78

Has the Vatican written
its own obituary?
(I mean literally.)
Its new Catechism
(cataclysm?)
pontificates
that punishment
should be
"proportional
to the gravity
of the crime,
without excluding
in extreme cases
the death penalty."

79

Vatican go boom

History repeats
      as farce, they say—
are fascists farcists
      in our day?

80

This all makes me sound
      like a grim little brat,
but somebody has to
      bell the Vat.

My name suggests
      I'm in line to try it—
so there you have it,
      my jeremiad.

81

Sword shares up, plowshares down

We're doing stories from the Bible,
    and after all these years it seems
the world is still so split and tribal,
    we're nowhere near the Prophets' dreams.

It's such a downer—when it's scanned
    by satellite from outer space,
you know the Earth's the Promised Land,
    you know we're all One Human Race.

82

World Economic Report

While there may be recession
    or even worse looming,
in the armaments sector
    business is booming.

83

Prophets are kicked
    down the nearest stair,
but profits are honored
    everywhere.

84

Prophets love their brethren—
    in turn, they smite 'em;
brethren and cistern
    are an item.

85

Prophets don't
    expect the Ritz,
but cisterns clearly
    are the pits.

86

Countries desire
    piles of loot,
but they need a prophet or two
    to boot.

87

They tend to be outcasts,
    truth to tell,
but then there's the case
    of Louis Riel.

Macdonald's regime
    sent a royal troop
to assure that he didn't
    stay out of the loop.

88

The Dalai Lama

He's gentle, wise,
    but, lacking puissance,
his cause, though just,
    is such a nuisance!

89

"The pen is mightier
 than the sword"—
a maxim massively
 ignored.

However, no one
 can rebut it;
the sword, we've seen,
 just doesn't cut it.

90

Assessing history's
 display,
the sword is pointless,
 strange to say.

91

R_x

When Moses came down
 from his mountain roost,
he brought two tablets
 he'd produced.

He saw a world
 in sorry plight;
"Take these", he said,
 "and you'll be all right."

Help yourself

He took the legends
    of primal tribes
and gave them universal
    vibes—

So that the whole world
    can rejoice,
appropriating
    his timeless voice.

For life abundant

He sought to empower
    the weak and meek—
"Justice, Justice
    shall you seek."

His Constitution
    (item four)
reached out beyond
    the human shore—

Enshrining thus
    his revelation:
a God of Love
    for our salvation.

No thoughts were wasted
    on the dead;
"Listen to the Earth"
    he said.

These are the very things
    that brand him—
no one wants to
    understand him.

94

"Nature, red
    in tooth and claw"
was not the Nature
    that he saw.

He saw the love,
    the freedom, play;
he called it "good"
    in every way.

95

He said that everyone's
    kin to each other,
and no one's better
    than another.

This revelation
    set man free,
and shakes the world
    continuously.

96

He rescued Health
    from superstition,
and placed it in
    our own volition:

Diet, rest,
    care, sanitation,
belief in goodness
    of Creation.

Peace on Earth, goodwill to all

He tried to decree
    a meatless diet,
but the freed tribespeople
    wouldn't buy it.

Manna was boring,
    though tasty and fresh—
they couldn't forget
    those pots of flesh.

(Food was everything
    in those days;
there was no TV,
    no films, no plays.)

They threatened rebellion—
    he had to bow—
it wasn't his time,
    his time is now.

Blood and Irony

Christmas, Passover,
    Eid Adha, grim
Thanksgiving—all
    derived from him—
What evil, fed
    by ignorant preachers—
holocausts
    of his pitied creatures.

Praise the Lord

To prevent himself being
    proclaimed a Messiah,
he cast himself into
    the role of pariah.

He arranged that his grave
    would be unknown—
worship belongs
    to God alone.

Individuals-R-Us

The Messiah business
    seems always humming
with First Appearance
    or Second Coming—

But it's not, in the long run,
    humanity's style,
be its cry Hosanna
    or Sieg Heil.

We feel our God-given brain's
    transcendence
through glorying in
    its independence.

"Saviors" are just
    too highly priced;
my human essence
    is antichrist.

Fantasy Math
(my kind of math)

The hypotenuse
    of the hippopotamus
is determined by measuring
    top to bottomus,
then dividing the width
    by the length of the tail,
and picking a card
    saying "Go to jail".

You roll the dice
    in a certain way,
and you're free to leave
    (providing you stay).
Now toss a coconut
    up in the air,
and watch where it lands.
    (No cheating. Be fair.)

The distance it falls
    away from your feet
will serve as a radius
    (after you eat).
Divvy it up
    with Sandy and Bruce,
and know what you've got?
    The hypotenuse!

I'm Me!

Most days you safely can assume
I'll hang my clothes, clean up my room,
but on occasion I'll become
a no-good putting-off-things bum.
My parents tell me there's two me's,
one born to frustrate, one to please,
but to myself, I'm still the same,
the only player in the game.
A leopard cannot change one spot,
but even if it could, so what?
A snake though putting on new skin
is still the same old snake within;
and if I'm not as nice as pie
sometimes,—it's still the same old I.

My Grandpa says,
    "If I did it over
I'd know the way
    to land in clover.

"But as it is
    I feel sort of beat,
winding up
    on uneasy street.

"In the game of life
    I was always tagged;
I always zigged
    when I should have zagged."

But *I* tell *him*
    that he's wrong, because
he's the best grandpa
    that there ever was.

105

My Uncle Sid's one of those comical guys,
he breaks Mom up till she almost cries;
but Dad says, "Though I agree he's affable,
spare me his jokes—I find them laughable."

106

"Sid said that his lawyer
        is quite a card;
he's in jail and he's hoping
        to be dis-barred."

But Dad completely
        refused to laugh;
"Not clever enough",
        he said, "by half".

107

My cousin Phil
        is kinda short,
and I have to admire
        his retort
when someone called him
        a "little runt":
"I'm taken aback
        by your affront."

108

Phil says, "I don't rock
    anyone's boat;
if you're looking to fight,
    I'll hold your coat.

"Sting like a butterfly,
    float like a bee—
that about says it
    for peaceable me.

"I owe this philosophy,
    in the main,
to a highly-developed
    sense of pain."

109

"Sometimes it hurts
    to duck away,
but not as much
    as if I'd stay.

"When I consider
    the case at length,
my cowardice
    is my greatest strength."

Mighty Mites
(by Cousin Phil)

I may not be Richard
    the Lion-hearted,
but I bear some resemblance
    to knights departed.

Though they challenged huge dragons
    and had what it takes,
they were challenged themselves
    in the stature stakes.

So perhaps even I
    might show militant zeal
if judiciously stashed
    in enough tons of steel.

"Outfitted thus,
    with sufficient pay,
working the knight shift
    might be okay."

"I'd need a sobriquet,
    not plain Phil;
would 'Philip the Mouse-hearted'
    fill the bill?"

113

Phil says, "Thank God
        we're sexual creatures—
it casts this glow
        on our fangy features—

"We don't see ourselves
        as food canals,
but as highly desirable
        guys and gals."

114

"On the coupling exchange,
        when I report,
I'll have no choice
        but to sell myself short."

115

Phil's been classed
        as a "gifted" kid—
he says the system
        has flipped its lid.

"Everyone's gifted—
        there's thousands of factors—
and those who label
        are gifted detractors."

116

Pedants in Wonderland
(by Cousin Phil)

Books are now rated
    according to ages—
Too old? Too young?
    Abjure those pages.

The "experts" have it
    all figured out—
except, that is,
    what it's all about.

117

I have this cousin Rhonda,
her heroine's Jane Fonda;
    she'll huff and puff
    to lose enough
to fit inside a Honda.

118

One exercise
    that she seems unable
to do, is pushups
    from the table.
She may be determined
    to lose that weight,
but she's striking out
    when she's at the plate.

What mostly sends her diet packing
is hot dogs, burgers, furtive snacking,
(fruits and veggies sadly lacking).

Uncle Sid says scads have died
from fast-food follies, fat and fried,
"But no one's ever yet been spied
committing, say, chop sueycide."

Oops!

Mom asked Rhonda
    to afternoon tea;
"I'm baking muffins,
    but count on me.

"And I'll be certain
    to bring a sample."
"Just bring yourself, dear,
    that'll be ample."

Big-otry

Appearances often
    deceive, it's true—
that bedrock wisdom's
    denied by few.

But when folks see Rhonda
    they look askance;
I can see that her entrance
    does not entrance.

122

When it comes to cousins
    and uncles and so,
everything's relative,
    don't you know.
And what exactly
    do I mean by that?
Just—I like them all,
    tall, thin or fat.
But on mulling over
    this teeming host,
Rhonda's the one
    I like the most.

123

My pony often licks me,
and he almost never flicks me;
    he runs like a rabbit,
    I christened him Habit,
and my Habit never kicks me.

My true best friend

He's not really a pony,
    he's a horse, you know,
when it comes to competing
    in a Western show.
His height just makes it
    to the "qualify" line,
resulting in ribbons
    for Jeremy Fine.

'Cause he's got a heart
    as big as the sky,
and nothing will make him
    bat an eye.
When it comes to running
    the obstacle courses,
he'll humble the biggest
    opposing horses.

I board him out
    at the "Circle O",
but I'm there as often
    as I can go.
He gallops to greet me
    like a long-lost friend,
and I know our friendship
    will never end.

When he's getting old
    and unable to run,
I'll look after him still,
    and we'll still have fun.
For the rest of his life
    I'll be there to see
the joy is returned
    that he brings to me.

125

My brother Ted is a speedy brat,
he dresses in thirty seconds flat;
I'm speedy too but wake up grumpy:
I do it in thirty seconds bumpy.

126

I asked him to wake me,
    since I sleep deeper;
he said, "Am I
    my brother's beeper?"

127

"What's for dessert?"
    cried my brother Ted;
"Chocolate mousse",
    my mother said.

"I'm not *that* hungry!
    I hate to grouse,
but could I just settle
    for a chocolate mouse?"

128

Ted's girlfriend Jill
    looked sad and strained;
men have no feelings,
    she complained.

Ted answered, "Jill,
    in all our dealings
we've clicked: but now
    you've hurt my feelings."

129

Ted promised her
    a precious stone
to show his love
    for her alone.

He sent a pebble
    from the beach;
he said it had
    triassic reach.

"Two hundred million
    years it's got:
is that a precious stone
    or what?"

130

A gold ring speaks
    to her demands—
she's into heavy
    metal bands.

131

The Noise Boys

My brother's band sure gets unwound,
they think that they invented sound.
You couldn't find a group that's prouder
    of getting lots of gig time,
and if they blast out any louder
    they're headed for the big time.

Scales strategy

How do they beat out
    every rival?
They depend on volume
    for survival.

Though his locks were purple
    and pink and green,
the drummer wanted
    to be more seen.

So he had them spiked
    like the punkers wear 'em;
he had it done
    at the *Hair'em-Scare'em*.

Pierced and bejewelled
    on every side,
he's still not holely
    satisfied.

A ring through his tongue
    is his next big plan—
"I've got to make
    my statement, man."

His name is Mule,
    and he told me once
in the great sex game
    he can be a dunce.

"I have lots of dates,
    but I'm not so slick
if I lay an egg
    when I'm with a chick.

"I'm like a craft
    without a rudder
as we feel our way
    around each other.

"It's a tricky sport
    and there's sure no cinches;
sex, I've learned,
    is a game of inches."

136

"Sex is like finance:
    withdrawals—a breeze,
but you don't make deposits
    with similar ease."

137

"The subject's replete
    with theory and hype;
I myself
    am a hands-on type."

138

"Sports: football, hockey,
    soccer, swimmin'—
they're not my thing,
    I'm into women."

139

"I look on sports
    with a certain loathing
(that is, the kind
    performed in clothing).

"I'm happy to bypass
    all that ouch
and do my scoring
    on a couch."

140

"Some guys like boobies,
    some like buns,
and most like both
    (your average ones).

"These outward parts
    deserve a mention,
but deeper things
    draw my attention."

141

"My formal education's
    slight,
but in my field
    I've done all right.

"I've scored a lot
    of *Thank you, ma'am*'s,
and never took
    entrance exams."

142

"It's a kind of war—
    the goal is glory
through occupying
    territory."

143

"Sometimes the action
    just sputters and stalls—
it's as though you're pitching
    with leaden balls.

"She's suddenly cold—
    I'm excited and shivery—
a case of all wind-up
    and no delivery."

144

"When I *do* score, I like it
    at least twice running,
but once I was barred
    from the second coming.

"'Soliciting *still?*' she said,—
    'Honey, no more of this!
I've made my donation,
    I gave at the orifice.'"

145

"It's best to pace things,
    brake, retard—
we all should do this,
    but it's hard."

146

"I've been to Britain,
    and I came to know
their sexual reticence
    just ain't so.

"France almost seems
    to have been their mentor,
their sex is so much
    front and center.

"They're hip to dozens
    of clever wiles
when it comes to laying 'em
    in the Isles."

147

"The men that women
    hate to know:
those feeling free
    to come and go."

148

"And we who stay
    are not exempt
from women's justified
    contempt.

"Dropping out
    should not, they scoff,
be prelude to
    our dropping off."

149

"Right now I'm young,
    and I'll be old—
I'm just a story
    told and told.

"The maple syrup
    pumps in Spring,
the baby bird
    fluffs out its wing,

"Ice melts, all Nature's
    on the go,
so why not let
    the juices flow?"

150

Ted's Song* (Splittin' Headache Howl)

I'm tired of bein' on the grievin' end,
the cleavin' end,
the heavin' end;
I wanna be on the receivin' end,
so don't 'spect nothin' from me.

No don't make up to me, don't pretend
to be my buddy, my pal, my friend,
all my crawlin' is gonna end,
so don't 'spect nothin' from me.

The givin' end ain't the livin' end,
it's the cryin' end,
the dyin' end;
I'm checkin' out of the lettin' end,
I'm gettin' onto the gettin' end,
so don't 'spect nothin' from me.

I'm tired of all the things that happen,
your prowlin', your yowlin', your yappin' and
        snappin',
I'd rather be rappin' than flappin' and scrappin',
it's new deal time for me.

You got boyfriends slinkin'
around at night,
ain't no way
I'm a-gonna fight,
maybe you're worth it,
but that's all right:
I'm lookin' after me.

---

*Ted's group, originally *The Racketeers*, then *The Screaming Egos*, is now *Bag O' Grosseries*. You may have heard them; if you're lucky, you may not have. (Just kidding.)

55

I was hooked on you, baby, a long, long time,
and it 'pears to me that it's time to climb,
clamber and scramble right outa the slime;
that's where I wanna be.
Oh, it had its good times while they lasted,
the reefers blissed us, the music blasted,
it sure got in your blood;
we were stroked and blended, coked and hashed,
zonked and skewered, stoned and smashed;
the highs were high but they only flashed,
the lows dragged on like mud.

But that's all over,
what I used to crawl for,
it's hard to give up
what you've given your all for,
it's cold out where you're free;
but that's okay: it's the cleavin' end,
goodbye to the cryin' and grievin' end,
I'm gonna be on the leavin' end,
I'm gonna swim out to sea;
I'm gettin' on the receivin' end
so don't 'spect nothin' from me,
no!
I'm gettin' on the receivin' end,
so don't 'spect nothin' from me,
no way!
No don't 'spect nothin',
don't 'spect nothin',
don't 'spect nothin' from me.
S'long babe.

Ted's Song Two (Regression Blues)

You say yes yes yes,
    you mean no no no,
you say stop stop stop,
    you mean go go go,
we can't get in sync,
    you're driving me wild,
you act like a little
    spoiled-rotten child;
Baby I'm yours,
    gonna make you mine,
gonna love you and hold you
    all the time.
If you wanna go back
    to when you were three,
don't be embarrassed,
    you can do it with me.

Regression!
Regression blues.
Ga-ga-ga's and goo-goo-goo's,
biddy-biddy-bum-bums and kitchy-kitchy-coos—
Regression!
Regression blues!

This mangy old world
    is a horrible place,
everyone conscripted
    in the old rat race;
Everyone's conforming
    to the tom-tom beat
but it comes from a computer
    and they think it's neat.
Baby stop that clock
    that's tickin' to the grave,
Go back! Go back!
    I'm your willing slave.

We don't have to follow
       in anyone's shoes,
we can make our own music,
       the regression blues.

Regression!
Regression blues.
Ga-ga-ga's and goo-goo-goo's,
biddy-biddy-bum-bums and kitchy-kitchy-coos—
Regression!
Regression blues!

152

Facing the music
       should be a snap,
but more and more
       it's a real bum rap.

153

I'm not bemoaning
       the fact we've got 'em,
but some of these bands
       have hit rock bottom.

154

Mad on ya

Some groups' deceptive
       tactics stink—
they charge for live
       and then lip-sync.

And look at all
       the loot they fetch!
These robber bands
       are sure a stretch.

155

Cruel choice?

If Sisyphus lived,
    would he be extolling
rolling rocks
    over rock 'n' rolling?

156

My auntie cries, "What luck!
We're going to dine on duck!"
    The duck appears
    to claps and cheers,
but all *I* say is: "Yuck".

Language Patrol

My sister Sue
    is at war with words;
a lot of our sayings
    are "for the nerds".
She gets into hassles
    with friends and teachers
over stamping out digs
    at our fellow creatures.

Like, sometimes to put off
    having a bath,
I'll ask her to help me
    do my math.
Whenever she won't
    she'll say that she
has "lots of bigger
    fish to free".

A coward could "human
    out" on you,
and "a bird in the bush
    is worth two in the zoo";
or she'll knit a sweater
    while on the phone,
and explain that she's "feeding
    two birds with one scone".

To belabor a point
    is to "flag a lead hearse",
and she even crusades
    against children's verse.
She warbles a song
    about "Three Kind Mice"
and the farmer's wife
    who treated them nice.

When she's at a party
  with folks "going grape",
she's sure to maneuver
  a quick escape.
But if things are sober
  and lots of fun,
she'll remain "until
  the last song is sung".

Say she saw somebody
  act like a goon:
she'd label them "crazy
  as a 'toon";
and when things go wrong
  she might "smell a brat",
but "There's more ways than one
  to cuddle a cat".

"Stubborn as a fool"
  and "a flake in the grass";
"dumb as a box"
  and "a silly sass";
"dirty as a rig",
  "cross as a boor"—
she's there for the animals,
  that's for sure.

I guess you could say
  she's a sort of saint,
except when you know her
  she really ain't.
But still and all,
  though we've often feuded,
she loves all creatures,
  me included.

Love 'em all

My Dad goes hunting in the Fall;
I don't agree with that at all;
my sister Sue, as you can guess,
is sympathetic even less.

When I saw *Bambi* I became
an "anti" in the hunting game;
they've all got mothers, just like me,
and that convinced me totally.

I'm one with feather, fin and fur,
I'm like the Ancient Mariner;
we studied it this year in school,
and man! I found it really cool.

Because he shot the albatross
he suffers loss on loss on loss,
until he learns to see the glory
in everything: and that's the story.

And if we're going to live in peace
our guns and such will have to cease;
it's not a question we abuse them,
if they're just *there* we're sure to use them.

There must be millions out there too
who think the same as me and Sue;
but still, it's sure not clear to all:
our Dad goes hunting in the Fall.

159

Poisoned wetlands

Hunters should
　　atone, redress,
as Wardens of
　　the Wilderness.

Instead of guns,
　　they'd have to head out
with spades, commanded
　　"Get the lead out!"

160

Young Miss Sprat
(by Sue)

"Jack Sprat would eat no fat,
　　His wife would eat no lean,
And so between the two of them
　　They picked the carcass clean."

Their daughter, watching this display,
　　turned every shade of green;
"I swear", she said, "that from this day
　　I'll eat nor fat *nor* lean."

Relighting a candle
(by Sue)

"God made all the creatures,
    and gave them our love and our fear,
To give sign, we and they are his children,
    one family here."
Browning wrote that
    in his typical poem *Saul*—
but who reads Browning these days?
    He's hardly remembered at all.
Let's conserve the treasures of man
    from neglect and derision;
to be truly conservative now
    is a liberal vision.

More from Sue (she's revving up)

'Course, some of what should be conserved
might cause us to become unnerved;
there's pretty potent stuff there: take
these limpid lines from William Blake:
"A robin redbreast in a cage
Puts all Heaven in a rage.
A dove-house filled with doves and pigeons
Shudders Hell through all its regions.
A dog starved at his master's gate
Predicts the ruin of the state.
A horse misused upon the road
Calls to Heaven for human blood."
And that was well before the days
of putting creatures in a maze
and shocking them with searing pain
to chart the time to go insane;
or strapping chimps on research beds
to test the force to crush their heads
by sadists we, to all our shame,
accord emoluments and fame.
If Blake is right (and look around,
no cause-effect appears more sound)
a day of reckoning is loomin'
for every proud uncaring human.

Vivisection
(by Sue)

Acids, knives, electrodes, clamps,
    and every kind of vile contrivance
to mutilate the living flesh—
    but that's okay, you see—it's "Science".

Local color
(by Sue)

Toronto has
    its claim to fame:
the *Noble-Collip*
    Drum, by name.

This thing's equipped
    with lethal bumps
against which its
    small victim thumps—

(A breather here
    for mice and rats—
drum science favors
    dogs and cats.)

A big strong human
    with a grin
stuffs the struggling
    creature in,

And 'round and 'round
    that chamber whirls,
and then the lab geeks
    mine their pearls

Of wisdom from
    the bloody mess,
to cheers from pulpit,
    pol and press.

The Draize Test
(by Sue)

Acid dripped
    in rabbits' eyes
often triggers
    a surprise:

The pain's so great
    from this attack
the clamped-in bunny
    breaks its back.

Amazing fact: torturers <u>lie</u>, too
(by Sue)

A bit concerned?
    They'll set you right;
Potemkin was
    a neophyte.

Listen up, frosh
(by Sue)

Location-wise
    you'll get a pass
if you assume
    the Ethics class

Is always held
    on another storey
from the animal-research
    lab'ratory.

Hell and high water
(by Sue)

"Conditioned reflex"
    was the rage
with Pavlov's tortured dogs
    on stage.

His pupil Stalin's
    realm comprised
the whole vast country
    Pavlovized.

Newton's Third
(or, What the media never tell us)
(by Sue)

How many millions
    of humans have died
when results of this "science"
    have been applied?
(The least of the lot
    is thalidomide—
that's just the one
    that they couldn't hide.)

The vivisecting Drug Trust
(by Sue)

The few reap wealth,
    the many, ill—
wealth versus health,
    a bitter pill.

171

Speaking of pushers . . .
(by Sue)

Something new
    in the global village:
pharmaceutical rape,
    or 'pillage'.

172

The vivisecting medical "researcher"
(or, Drug Trust Doughboy)
(by Sue)

The oath he took
    might cause alarm—
that little matter
    of "no harm"—

But one (he says)
    must sink or swim—
he reads it as
    no harm to *him.*

Drug Trust butchery
(by Sue)

If animal torture
    is truly the answer,
how come growing
    rates of cancer?

The drug-pumped media
    soothe the mourner:
"Success is just
    around the corner."

By the time they've really
    hit their stride,
we'll have *all* succumbed
    to pharmacide.

Drug Trust R_x
(by Sue)

Indication:
    drawing breath.
Contraindication:
    death.

"Torture of animals,
        Shakespeare remarks,
has a single consequence:
        hardened hearts.

"That's why, though they know
        its results are for fools,
they teach that torture
        in medical schools."

"That way, they're assured
        a steady supply
of docs who will not
        bat an eye

"At clandestine
        experiments
on institutional
        residents."

"I'm glad to be able
        to alert you;
what you don't know
        can really hurt you."

A book for the ages
(by Sue)

A seminal publishing
      event:
Slaughter of
    the Innocent.

The phony "animal
      welfare" groups
that protect the flanks
      of the Drug Trust troops

Despise and fear
      the Hans Ruesch name—
they've learned how it feels
      to be "fair game".

I read a poem . . .
(by Sue)

I read a "poem"
   the other day
as great as any
   that's come my way.

It throbs like a pulsar,
   it beams as a guide
to a sane, humane world . . .
   . . . you decide.

* * *

The famous example of former President Hoover's stringent logic, "When many workers are out of a job, unemployment ensues", is to be found again and again in the scientific protocols: "When food is withheld from a living organism, starvation ensues. We have proved it scientifically on a statistically significant number of dogs, cats, monkeys, donkeys, pigs, and other animals, and are prepared to prove it again, provided the grants keep coming."

But today, not even such flimsy pretexts are being invoked by the majority of those people who conduct what they have named "basic research". Basically, it consists of getting hold of healthy animals and destroying them physically and mentally through the infliction of gratuitous torments that a morally sane individual would not even be able to conceive, let alone execute.

—Hans Ruesch, *Naked Empress or The Great Medical Fraud* (CIVIS Publications, 1986)

Hans Ruesch, Immortal
(by Sue)

More powerful than
    all man-made laws:
a great, great writer
    with a great, great cause.

The voice of the voiceless—
    including us;
we're butchered too
    by the weird Drug Trust.

Our bemused descendants
(by Sue)

They'll scratch their heads
    without having itches—
same as we do
    about burning witches.

John Brown's soul
(by Sue)

This is no issue
    for quiet debate—
torture's the issue
    that cannot wait—

Those who rip open
    the torture-lab's door
war on the evil
    heart of war.

"But let's be clear—
    as soon as we enter,
alarms will go off
    in Rock Feller Center—

"The Drug Trust will pull
    its thousand strings
and come a-bombing
    on angels' wings."

Dreaming of Genes with Light Brown Hair
(by Sue)

We have our modern
    Frankensteins,
spinning their
    eugenic lines.

They want to neatly
    pile on shelves
replicas
    of their warped selves.

And—further tribute
    to their brain—
"create" new life forms
    fleshed in pain.

Means and Ends
(by Sue)

It's all one issue
    from Nome to Perth—
erasing torture
    from this Earth.

Being human
(by Sue)

A truck passed me by
    on a day that was hotter
than hell, with a cargo
    slated for slaughter.

They were packed so tight
    some must have been dead
by the time they arrived
    at the killing shed.

I demand to be spared
    such acts and sights—
I'll fight to the death
    for my human rights.

Holocaust
(by Sue)

It isn't far
    from truck to train,
and "cattle cars"
    invade my brain.

Some folk may find
    the notion risible,
but cruelty
    is indivisible.

"Rosa Luxemburg
　　was jailed
and wondered why
　　the movement failed.

"One day she watched
　　as cruel force
was brought against
　　a struggling horse,

"And not through any
　　social stance,
but just from species
　　arrogance.

"That made her understand,
　　she said,
the long, long road
　　that lay ahead."

Death of a Heroine
(by Sue)

The jockey was whipping her
    hard and long
before the massive
    cheering throng.

Then her foreleg snapped
    with a sickening crack—
you could hear it all around
    the track.

There were cries of rage
    and a few of glee—
(she was the favorite,
    you see).

A blizzard of tickets
    filled the air,
as gamblers vented
    their despair.

They shot her, of course,
    but out of view,
then sold her off
    for leather and glue.

Crime and Punishment
(by Sue)

The circus arrives—
    behind the stage
is an elephant (chained)
    and a bear in a cage.

The cage is tiny—
    there's hardly room
to turn around
    in that fetid gloom.

His jailers feed him
    and keep him warm;
he's let out only
    to perform.

With teeth filed down
    and claws cut out,
he's the starring clown
    in a boxing bout.

Parents bring children
    to cheer and hiss.—
What fate should befall us
    for crimes like this?

Bullfight: papal blessing
(by Sue)

A torture-necklace
    of steel-barbed thorns—
Who'll take the devil
    by the horns?

Man's dominion
(by Sue)

Gather 'round, folks,
    and hear my lay,
how the passenger pigeon
    passed away.

They were here by the billion,
    flying high;
witnesses say
    they darkened the sky.

But with man around
    they were out of luck;
the passenger pigeon
    was a sitting duck.

We got every last one
    of the passenger race,
but we keep those guns cocked
    just in case.

Buffalo Bill
(by Sue)

When Buffalo Bill
    tracked down a "stand",
no happier honcho
    trod the land.

He shot and shot,
    they tottered and tottered,
resignedly waiting
    their turn to be slaughtered.

The only thing
    that slowed him down
was the gunpowder smoke
    clouding the ground.

It was *the* best sport
    on the Western Plain—
"Sure beats shootin'
    from a moving train."

Ol' Bill did well
    for the cattle trust—
millions of bison
    bit the dust.

Buffalo Bill:
    one of the greats;
they'll never forget him
    down in the States.

194

"There's money in animals,
　　if you're willing—
any moron
　　can make a killing."

195

And the beat goes on
(by Sue)

"Oh give me a home
where the buffalo roam,
　　and the deer and the antelope play,
and a fridgeful of brew,
and an Uzi or two,
　　it's a blast in the U.S. of A."

So sang the fantasizing lad,
　　afoot for burger, coke and fries,
what time a hapless ricochet
　　cut short his dream of paradise.

196

"A lot of hunters
　　bag each other,
incidents
　　the newcasts smother.

"A question that
　　this harvest poses:
do trophies rate
　　by ears, or noses?"

"Some hunters claim
    they love their prey
in a religious
    sort of way.

"An arrow through
    a doe's bright eye
connects, they brag,
    with the Most High.

"A sick joke, meant
    to fog the harms
that flow from ever-
    lasting arms."

Loyalty
(by Sue)

A petting zoo
    toured 'round the malls—
lambs, calves, piglets
    in their stalls—

Playful, trusting
    baby goats—
fondle them,
    then slit their throats.

"Blood, blood, blood—
    what bloody insanity!
There's something rotten
    in the state of humanity."

The blood is the life
(by Sue)

The killing is endless—
    hour by hour
Earth is drenched
    in a bloody shower.

And cancer, hunger,
    war, plague, blight,
have causes still unknown?
    Yeah, right.

"The way things alter
    is alarmin',
but here's a rock
    you can bet the farm on:

"Two plus two
    is always four—
never less
    and never more."

The Good Samoyed
(by Sue)

A precept we
    profess to favor:
Leviticus's
    "Love your neighbor".
A scream awakened me
    from nappin',
and this is how
    I saw it happen:

A girl lay sprawled,—
    a man on top
was punching her—
    he wouldn't stop.
People passed
    and looked away;
I too was stunned,
    I'm 'shamed to say.

When suddenly,
    where no one dared,
a white Samoyed,
    fangs all bared,
swept like a ghost
    across the road,
unfazed as rush-hour
    traffic flowed.

And in an instant,
    silently,
the man was down,
    the woman free.
Then people stopped
    to lend assistance,
now that the man
    showed no resistance.

And giving just
        a little cough,
the Good Samoyed
        trotted off,
seeking no payment
        for his labor—
God's masterpiece,
        who loved his neighbor.

203

In a word . . .
(by Sue)

"You stole, raped and murdered—
        let me not fudge:
You behaved like an *animal*!"
        quoth the judge.

204

It's all around us
(by Sue)

We brag about
        "the human spirit"
to such excess
        I wince to hear it.
Homer, that
        immortal guy,
praised "the courage
        of a fly."

Homage to Homer
(by Grandpa)

Homer the sanctified—
    what a misnomer!
Read him, discover
    the humor of Homer.

It's there to disturb,
    delight, upend—
the subtlest irony
    ever penned.

Savage boar, wonderful people
(Sue gives us a story from Homer, Iliad, *Book 9)*

When Oeneus,
    the Aetolian king,
failed at harvest-time
    to bring
offerings to
    great Artemis,
the goddess took
    offense at this,
and loosed a monstrous
    white-tusked boar
who tramped his orchards,
    even tore
whole apple trees
    up by the roots,
to raven down
    the luscious fruits.

Oeneus' city
    of Calydon
couldn't supply
    sufficient brawn
to tackle this
    ferocious monster,
abetted by
    its heavenly sponsor.
So Meleager,
    Oeneus' pride
(his son), recruited
    from far and wide
a legion of princes
    to go to war
against this monstrous
    savage boar.

Now notwithstanding
        divine decree,
this elite host
        gained victory.
Many thrusts were made,
        but the fatal one
was by Meleager,
        the king's brave son.

But Artemis wasn't
        finished yet—
she knew her business
        and she set
the victors fighting
        for head and pelt,
prizes of honor
        deeply felt.
Thus: Meleager
        wished to grant a
prize to huntress
        Atalanta,
whose arrow hit
        a vital part,
but more, his own
        lust-smitten heart.
But Plexippus,
        the bold Curetian
(his uncle), stopped
        his fellow Grecian,
and said, "the prize
        is rightly mine."
Meleager's spear
        sliced through his spine.
Another uncle
        intervened;
he too was fatally
        demeaned.

Well! Now we have
    a bloody war,
enraged men meting out
    what-for.
But here's a switch:
    Meleager's mother's
aghast at losing
    her two brothers,
and bids the hellish
    Furies take
her son to Hades
    for her sake.
This mother's curse
    inflamed his brain;
he swore he'd never
    fight again,
retiring to
    his sleeping-room,
and leaving Calydon
    to its doom.

While thus eschewing
    further strife,
he had for company
    his wife,
the lovely Cleopatra.
    I
feel obligated
    to supply
her pedigree:
    her father's name
was Idas, he
    of fighting fame.
In later days
    Meleager died,
and Cleopatra
    cried and cried,

and mourned so constantly,
    her father
believed her name—
    or nickname, rather—
should be "Halcyonē"
    because
her grief, so unremitting,
    was
akin to that
    which is often heard
when her mate is mourned
    by the halcyon bird.

But back to our tale.
    Meleager brooded
on his mother's curse,
    abed, denuded,
uncaring of
    his city's fate,
while the battle raged
    at Calydon's gate.

Now the Council comes
    to his sealed-off room,
begs him to heed
    the city's doom,
offers him huge
    awards of land—
in vain: he will not
    lift a hand.
Now his father knocks
    and pleads his due,
and lo and behold,
    his mother too.
At the sight of *her*
    he sets his teeth;
his sword grows cobwebs
    in its sheath.

He managed to stay
　　unmoved, aloof,
till missiles crashed
　　through the bedroom roof;
the Curetians had breeched
　　the outer wall—
houses were burning—
　　the town would fall!
Then Cleopatra
　　sobs and pleads,
reminding him
　　of the sacker's deeds,
the rape, the pillage,
　　blood and flame—
he stirs, he rises,
　　stung by shame.

He buckles his armor on,
　　grabs his sword,
and puts to flight
　　the Curetian horde!
Calydon's saved!
　　They've won the war!
　　　. . .
And that's the story
　　of the savage boar.

207

Critique by Grandpa

A perfect example
　　of Homer's art—
there's something beneath
　　the story part—
an undercurrent
　　of new direction
you can sail along
　　through introspection.

2800 years later—Are we really so smart?
(by Grandpa)

Homer's characters
    wouldn't know
an abstract thought
    if it bit their toe.

Everything's visual,
    concrete, real;
the gods are spokes
    in the same crude wheel.

(And broken spokes,
    if truth be told;
Homer's irony
    left them cold.)

There's no talk of fashion,
    cuisine, art;
even money
    has yet to start.

No childhood analysis,
    introspect stuff,
whether life
    had been kind or rough.

Description of features,
    too, is nil—
"ugly", "beautiful",
    fill the bill.

(Used, of course,
    as ironic jollities;
Homer's concern
    is inner qualities.)

Not fertile ground
      for characters, eh?
What in the world
      would they find to say?

And yet they've never
      been outdated;
they're as real today
      as the day created.

That's the only test
      that counts, I fear;
how many characters
      last a year?

You can talk psychology
      night and day,
but the proof of the pudding,
      as they say . . .

What does this tell
      about incidentals
ranged alongside
      fundamentals?

And what those fundamentals
      are—
that's the cold
      unreachable star.

So compared to Homer
      how do you rate your
"up-to-date" knowledge
      of human nature?

If only they could speak . . .
If only we could see . . .
(Sue presents a tale from Moses, Numbers 22)

Though Balaam the seer
    believed that his God
had told him to go
    where the Moabite trod,
the Lord had a different
    purpose in mind,
which you'll read about here,
    if you feel so inclined.

He mounted his donkey,
    himself and his load,
but God sent an angel
    to stand in the road
and interdict passage
    with fiery sword—
"Thus far and no farther",
    a sign from the Lord.

But Balaam the seer
    was blind to the fact;
he urged on his donkey
    so heavily packed.
The donkey, however,
    perceived she must yield,
and patiently plodded
    aside to the field.

Now Balaam's accustomed
    to being obeyed
by four-legged creatures
    who serve till they're flayed.
He takes up his cudgel
    and beats the poor beast,

till she figures the angel
        will harm her the least.

Back she adventures,
        and, finding the path
deserted now, blesses
        the cooling of wrath.
But now the road narrows,
        stone fence either side,
a perfect arrangement
        for danger to hide.

And sure enough, there,
        just a little way off,
stood the angel, sword raised,
        where the road hit a trough.
The donkey's heart thumped—
        she must somehow go through—
there was fear from all sides—
        what to do? what to do?

She gathered her courage
        and pressed hard against
the edge of the road,
        though impregnably fenced.
And wonder of wonders
        she got past the sword,
but scraped the bare foot
        of her sensitive lord.

Balaam's enraged now,
        he's howling with pain,
he curses the donkey
        and beats her again.
Bruised, cut and bleeding,
        she plods bravely on,
her only complaint
        an inaudible moan.

And now comes the climax!
    She sinks to her knees!
The angel stands guard
    where there's no room to squeeze!
She knows what will come,
    she feels pinioned and trussed,
but all her great spirit
    accepts what it must.

Her master descends
    from the brave creature's back,
and blindly resumes
    his ferocious attack.
He's screaming with fury:
    "Make fun of me, will you?
If I had me a sword here
    I'd instantly kill you!"

But now the compassionate
    Lord of Creation
accords the poor donkey
    the gift of oration.
"Am I still not the very
    same creature you've tasked
for so many years,
    who's done all that you've asked?

"Have I ever once acted
    before in this way?
Have you known me to ever,
    just once, disobey?
Have I ever once even
    been tardy or slow?"
Old Balaam was dumbfounded,
    murmuring, "No."

Then the Lord of Creation
        unsealed Balaam's eyes—
he saw the armed angel,
        he gasped his surprise;
he fell to the ground
        with his face in the dust
to show his allegiance,
        his fear, hope and trust.

And the angel accosted him
        harshly, and said
"Three times I cried halt
        but you forged straight ahead.
Had your donkey you beat
        with such cruelty, not
had the good sense to turn,
        you were dead on the spot.

"Yes, I would have destroyed you",
        the angel went on,
"Be sure you remember
        these words when I'm gone.
I would have destroyed you,
        three times I aver;
you owe your poor life
        not to me, but to her."

Cruel Nature
(by Sue)

Nature
is so
incredibly cruel
that
when you take
one of its creatures
out
of its
natural
environment,
it wants nothing more
than
to
return
to it.

I thought you might entertain
a vignette or two
illustrating common,
typical
procedures
of Nature's
cruellest
beast.

* * * * *

Through the years I have got to know a number of
leopards, although not so well as this mother and her
cub. Each individual is recognizable by its spots and
so, whenever I see a lady with a leopard skin coat,
I can't help peering at it to see if I knew the leopard.
I am also curious to know if the skin has any flaws.

If not I wonder if it came from a certain dealer in Nairobi, who was seen to kill a leopard by holding it immobile in a crushcage, a cage the sides of which can be moved inwards, and then sticking a red hot poker up its anus.

—Hugo van Lawick, *Savage Paradise;*
  The Predators of Serengeti

To cook a live lobster, bring salted water (use two tablespoons of salt per quart of water) to a boil. There should be enough water to completely cover the lobster. Hold the lobster by its back and plunge it head first into the water. Cover and return to a boil. Lower heat to a bubbling simmer and cook 12 to 20 minutes, depending on size. The lobster is done when an antenna comes free easily.

—Canadian Press (*The Toronto Star*,
  May 11, 1994)

Just thinking
(by Sue)

Those who bring torture
    to living creatures
might ponder two of life's
    salient features:

Action and reaction
    balance the scale,
and nobody sees
    beyond the veil.

That hook in the mouth,
    that lab from hell—
could the creature be *you*?
    Time will tell.

212

"We ask for mercy—
    in God we trust—
but we show no mercy
    when God is *us*."

God of Love
(by Sue)

We console ourselves
    we're in the hands
of a merciful God
    who understands.

But "merciful God"'s
    just a shibboleth
if creatures are made
    to be tortured to death.

We impact the question:
    that which *we* crave,
if we don't give,
    how can we have?

Whirlwind Ramble
(by Sue)

Job was a just man
    in his own view,
and he did try hard
    when the world was new.

But he had blind spots
    of massive size,
and God set out
    to open his eyes.

But the catch is, God
    can't be direct—
free will, you know—
    so, circumspect.

Out of the whirlwind
    he dashed Job's hope,
sounding a bit
    like a misanthrope.

Job couldn't read
    between the lines,
but surely we can
    in these latter times.

"You think you're the greatest,
    little man?
Meet Behemoth
    and Leviathan.

"You think I only
    have eyes for you?
I love the fawn,
    the vulture too.

"You do terrible things
        in my commonweal—
you pierce soft flesh
        with cruel steel.

"The tools of torture—
        hook, ring, whip, chain—
you spare no pains
        inflicting pain.

"You can't claim goodness
        and be abusive;
mercy and justice
        are not exclusive.

"Hate and cruelty
        run their course,
always rebounding
        against the source."

Job heard the words
        but missed the point;
the world's still sadly
        out of joint.

We inherit the faith,
        let's learn and keep it;
we'll heed the whirlwind
        or we'll reap it.

Dominion Day
(by Sue)

Let's set aside
    a day to feel
our vile dominion,
    and to heal.

To turn our faces
    to the Garden,
smash the guns
    and beg for pardon.

The life that trembles
    at our sight
alone can lead us
    to the light.

216

Sue's glad that fur
    is becoming passé;
she thought she'd never
    see the day.

"But it isn't over—
    let's keep the war on;
'humane trapping'—
    what an oxymoron!"

217

Why me?
(by Sue)

Escape from a trap
    is hard to *bring* off—
the leg must be sacrificed
    (called a "wring-off").

When they find these stumps,
    the trappers swear
their lot in life
    just isn't fair.

218

"I never dispute
    with the fur lobby chaps;
I'm the first to concede
    they've got minds like steel traps."

Le Canada, Eh
(A "One Founding Creator" Story)
(by Sue)

> His*tender mercies are over all his works.
> — *Psalm* 145:9

Well it's a darn big land and it's kind of neat
how the Lord made the world but it wasn't
      complete,
and she looked around and she said "Aha!
Voici l'endroit pour le Canada!"
And she took the best from the bright blue sea,
and the purest air and the tallest tree,
and the richest gifts from her deepest stores
made our country's ores.

Chorus: Well Canada you're the planet's jewel,
            Canada yeah yeah yeah!
            It's the treasure trove of the God of love,
            it's our kinder gentler Canada.
            Le Canada vert d'une mer à l'autre,
            le Canada, nous sommes là!
            You can live in peace when you've got
               a lease
            on Canada.

And the Lord said "Now that I've made this land
gotta give some thought to the proper brand
of life to shape it, smart and eager",
so she made the little beaver.
And the beavers did their work, and the moose
      came along,

---

*The psalmist employs the masculine pronoun, but there are
Biblical instances of feminine imagery in reference to the
Creator. Following that example, I have combined the
masculine "Lord" and "God" with the feminine pronouns.

then people she chose who were bright and strong,
First Nations people, Hip Hurrah
for our Canada!

Chorus: Well Canada etc.

And the Lord rejoiced in the land's allure,
and she said "Cette terre est une terre d'amour,
and all the creatures from my hand
gonna live in peace in a peaceful land."
And she guided the ships and she opened the doors,
and the people sailed in from their crowded shores,
and her beautiful animals filled their part
of our country's heart.

Chorus: Well Canada you're the planet's jewel,
         Canada yeah yeah yeah!
         It's the treasure trove of the God of love,
         it's our kinder gentler Canada.
         Le Canada vert d'une mer à l'autre,
         le Canada, nous sommes là!
         We can thrive in peace if we guard
              our lease
         on Canada.

Le Canada, Eh

Music by David Walden

1. Well it's a darn big land and it's kind of neat how the Lord made the world but it

wasn't complete, and she looked around and she said "Aha! Voici l'endroit

pour le Canada!" And she took the best from the bright blue sea, and the purest air and the

tallest tree, and the richest gifts from her deepest stores made our country's ores. Well

CHORUS:

Canada you're the planet's jewel, Canada yeah yeah yeah! It's the treasure trove of the

God of love, it's our kinder gentler Canada. Le Canada vert d'une mer à l'autre, le

Canada, nous sommes là! You can live in peace when you've got a lease on Ca - na - da.

The death of Redruff
(from Redruff, the story of the Don Valley[*] partridge, by Ernest Thompson Seton)[**]
(presented by Sue)

One by one the deadly cruel gun had stricken his near ones down, till now, once more, he was alone. The Snow Moon slowly passed with many a narrow escape . . .

It seemed, at length, a waste of time to follow him with a gun, so when the snow was deepest, and food scarcest, Cuddy hatched a new plot. Right across from the feeding-ground, almost the only good one now in the Stormy Moon, he set a row of snares. A cottontail rabbit, an old friend, cut several of these with his sharp teeth, but some remained, and Redruff, watching a far-off speck that might turn out a hawk, trod right in one of them, and in an instant was jerked into the air to dangle by one foot.

Have the wild things no moral or legal rights? What right has man to inflict such long and fearful agony on a fellow-creature, simply because that creature does not speak his language? All that day, with growing, racking pains, poor Redruff hung and beat his great, strong wings in helpless struggles to be free. All day, all night, with growing torture, until he only longed for death. But no one came. The morning broke, the day wore on, and still he hung there, slowly dying; his very strength a curse. The second night crawled slowly down, and when, in the dawdling hours of darkness, a great Horned Owl, drawn by the feeble flutter of a dying wing, cut short the pain, the deed was wholly kind.

---

[*]The Don Valley is an ageless treasure of Metropolitan Toronto, and today part of its acreage bears the name E. T. Seton Park in memory of the great Canadian naturalist, painter, writer, conservationist, feminist, fervent admirer of the First Nations peoples and creator of the Boy Scouts (originally the Woodcraft Indians) and the Girl Guides. His books still sell in the millions around the world. A true prophet, Seton is not much honored in his home country (apart from the park).

[**]*Redruff* is one of the stories in *Wild Animals I Have Known*, (1898). In his introduction, Note to the Reader, Seton has this to say:

These stories are true . . . Redruff really lived in the Don Valley north of Toronto, and many of my companions will remember him. He was killed in 1889 . . . I hope some will herein find emphasized a moral as old as scripture—we and the beasts are kin. . . . . Since, then, the animals are creatures with wants and feelings differing in degree only from our own, they surely have their rights. This fact, now beginning to be recognized by the Caucasian world, was first proclaimed by Moses and was emphasized by the Buddhist over 2,000 years ago.

My Grandpa says,
    "I was never a saver;
my philosophy was,
    if I had 'er, I gave 'er.

"There's no sense in hoarding,
    you might as well spend it,
bestow it, bestrew it,
    gamble it, lend it.

"It's the sinews of life,
    but why amass it?
Since life itself
    is a wasting asset.

"But somehow it's longer
    than one had thought,
and the days of living
    must still be bought."

My Grandpa says,
    "As one gets older,
messengers of time
    grow bolder.

"The body's guardians
    take wing,
the cells no longer
    do their thing.

"Memory lags,
    reactions slow,
functions all
    are stop-and-go.

"The balance
    on the other side
is life experience
    deep and wide.

"They rate it highly
    at the banks,
and will accept it
    with their thanks."

Because he's concerned with life's brevity,
my Dad devours books on longevity;
    but between what he knows
    and the way that he goes
there's a gap that invites my Mom's levity.

223

My Mom told my Dad,
    "Though I must dissent,
there's a germ of truth
    in your argument."

My Dad replied,
    "In my whole polemic
only a germ?
    No! An epidemic!"

My Mom responded,
    "You exaggerate vastly!
Your argument, dear,
    was not *that* ghastly!"

224

Dad takes a call

"Are you the head
    of the family Fine?"
asked the voice at the other
    end of the line.

"Head? I wish
    I were feeling more so;
in actual fact
    I'm more like the torso."

Here's Dad!

Jeremy asked me
    to write a pome
"to give my book
    the flavor of home."

I can't write for blazes,
    and that's in prose;
when it comes to poetry,
    up your nose.

But I can't escape it,
    I'm everyone's vassal;
the flavor of home?
    Right: a home's a man's hassle.

The Pessimist

My Dad declares,
"Though my stocks are declining,
I read that it's bright
    for the longer pull;
which shows that the lack
of a bull in the market
in no way depresses
    the market for bull."

Dad's Lament

We sweat and strain
    to make our money,
and when we have it
    we treat it funny.

We agonize
    for a place to park it,
and the gains of the marketplace
    lose in the market.

"The whole darn market
    is much too high;
it'll keep on falling,"
    said Dad with a sigh.

"I wouldn't have bought
    if I'd been astuter;
it's projecting earnings
    way into the future."

"The future?" Uncle Sid
    said with laughter;
"Not only the future,
    but the Hereafter!"

Stock Talk
(by Dad)

We're like those puppets
    on a string,
jerked around
    like anything.

We leap to buy them
    when they jump,
and sell the suckers
    when they slump.

Whipsawed between
    despair and greed,
we come with bleeding
    guaranteed.

230

"If you want to see
    a stockbroker frown,
casually ask him
    'What's goin' down?'"

231

A blizzard blew,
    but Dad succeeded
in going to work,
    though Mom sure pleaded.

She cried, "I wish
    that I could ground you,
but keep the car
    wrapped well around you."

232

My Mom's as super
    as they come;
Dad tells me she's
    the maxi-mom.

233

To wash, cook, care,
    clean the abode—
these constitute
    the mother load.

234

Impugn the family?
    We daren't;
it's the place where God
    makes love apparent.

We've had mishaps driving
    from here to there
'cause Dad forgets
    to fix the spare.

Mom is goaded
    to use invective,
but Grandpa puts it
    in perspective.

"So we don't spend too much
    time regretting,
the mind's formidable
    at forgetting.

"Thus wounds can heal,
    spirits renew;
but the Law of Downside
    applies here too:

"Since the mind doesn't care
    what it lays to rest,
slips that should caution us
    get repressed.

"So we find ourselves often
    with more than our share of
recurring mistakes
    we should be aware of.

"Then we call ourselves stupid,
    and slap our foreheads,
and wish we had
    a couple of more heads.

"But every time
      you repeat a flub,
you're just being human—
      join the club."

236

Earth hosts a feast
      that never sates;
it serves it on
      tectonic plates.

237

I read about things that have died
      and the thousands of species just vanishing;
I don't feel much pride
and at last I decide
      that it's *us* that the Earth should be banishing.

238

If *I* were a species
      under man's sway,
I'd opt for extinction
      any day.

239

For Heaven's sake

They say that today there is *no* zone
that's a freedom-to-healthily-grow zone;
      there's a hole in the sky
      that could make us all fry;
what we need is a Wizard of Ozone.

Fumes of doom

The protective covering
    might unravel,
but that's an airy-fairy
    cavil
when weighed alongside
    jet-plane travel.

Our love affair
    with Earth, may be
terminating
    rapidly—
it lacks the proper
    chemistry.

Global warning

Pheidippides sounded
    a wake-up call,
Laura Secord
    tipped a brawl,
Americans
    revere their Paul—
but Chicken Little
    tops them all.

243

No problem repairing
    the ozone stratum—
look at our record
    with the atom—

Our nuclear journey,
    though rather short,
has already earned us
    a glowing report.

244

Touched, I'm sure

Dupont, Westinghouse,
    you and me—
just one big nuclear
    family.

245

Nuclear warheads:
    a vile statistic;
it should be making us
    go ballistic.

246

Mother Nature wields big sticks

One thing we've got lots of is trees,
in the Fall there are leaves to our knees;
    but you can't have enough
    of that natural stuff
or the planet will sizzle or freeze.

Sound Philosophy

If a tree falls in the forest
    when there's not a soul around,
philosophers can speculate
    it may not make a sound—

But what we know for certain is,
    when *we* commit the felling
the decibel effect is huge
    'cause more and more are yelling.

Chainsaw Massacre
(Clayoquot Sound)

It doesn't matter
    how old and rare,
Corporate interests
    just don't care.

A pity the power
    to make the rules
lies in the hands
    of lumbering fools.

Job losses? Well,
    you can call me a louse,
but who'd sell the farm
    to be renting the house?

Or who would contend
    that it might be the norm
to burn your house down
    to ensure that you're warm?

History shows
    this is more than just hopin':
closing a bad door
    lets ten good ones open.

What exactly is
    an economy
if not soil, water
    air and tree?

Clear, you say?

Famed for bestowing
    hugs and kisses
upon himself
    was young Narcissus.

The face and form
    that made him drool
he saw reflected
    in a pool.

This tale will stump
    the future hearer—
what, water acting
    as a mirror?

We took a field trip to the zoo,
I found it sad and you would too;
with all the ways we humans bungle,
I'm giving three cheers for the jungle.

If tigers open up a store
it should be basic, nothing more;
their operation should, by law,
be classified a maw and paw.

254

I follow the saga
    of the whooping crane;
they may never be seen
    on Earth again.

But they may just make it,
    though painful and slow;
the flock has reached
    a hundred or so.

Too late, we cherish
    this soulful troop;
no regular crane
    will ever whoop.

255

Gorillas in the Abyss

The last few hundred
    are doomed to go—
the world's a marketplace,
    you know.

And there's nothing like
    gorilla hands
for making showpiece
    ashtray stands.

A metaphor
　　we perhaps should drop:
the bull inside
　　a china shop.

It's trumped by an image
　　before our eyes:
humans in Earth's
　　trashed paradise.

I think you'll agree,
　　if you properly scan it,
we had here a bonafide
　　world-class planet.

The James Bay Cree
　　are crying foul,
and they swear they won't
　　throw in the towel.

And I'm with them in spirit
　　as I swim at our cottage;
what, sell our birthright
　　for a mess of wattage?

Cold-hearted War
(NATO playground)

Jets screeching treetop-level
      pin you
to the ground—
      and if you're Innu

It happens forty
      times a day—
but for your own
      protection, eh?

What's fittin'

Fashion is foreign
      to us Greens;
we're really not into
      dominant jeans.

As long as it isn't
      fur or leather,
we don't have trouble
      getting it together.

Non-designer labels
      suit us fine;
just wrapping our buns
      is our bottom line.

As Time Goes By

An occurrence one
      shouldn't bet one's stash on—
Fashion itself
      going out of fashion.

Fashion Lords

Women-hating
    men conspire
to drape their dupes
    in their sattire.

For our own good
(by Cousin Rhonda)

Mother Nature
    and Father Time
are the subjects
    of my rhyme:

Two stern parents
    who decree
a slippery slope
    for vanity.

"Grooming's not something
    to stamp our foot on,
but make-up? Well,
    that's just a put-on."

Those who fight
    against control
of population
    play a role

That planet Earth
    cannot abide;
it's planning
    or it's planetcide.

Message from Earth
(Pope-ulation crisis)

My stressed digestive
    system's full;
I can swallow no more
    of that papal bull.

Our sojourn on Earth
    has been nightmarish,
but delivered its message:
    Cherish or perish.

268

What's my religion?
     This blue Eden;
Earth and its Maker
     are all we're needin'.

Let others blanch
     at hellish furies,
or visualize
     those heavenly houris.

To me it's all
     exceedingly odd;
I'll put my faith
     in a loving God.

269

Eternity sounds
     like an awful prize;
that's the paradox
     of Paradise.

Happy Mortality

"Eternal life?
       Sure I believe!
Don't we all?"
       said my cousin Steve.

"Here, everything ends;
       in that new dawn
things will go on
       and on and on . . .

"And on and on
       and on and (yawn)
on and on
       and on and on . . .

" . . . I'm starting to think,
       when I pass that portal
I'll beg and plead
       to remain a mortal."

A Dream
(of a forgetful angel)

"Heaven is closed",
       the angel said,
"we can't afford
       the overhead.

"You'll have to find heaven
       where we give you birth,
which means this beautiful
       planet . . . um . . .

whichever one you're on at the moment."

Yin/Yang
(by Grandpa)

Sometimes we have
  the mental leaning
that death deprives
  life of its meaning.

But the truth of the matter
  is just the reverse:
the meaning of life
  is the death we curse.

The Book of Job
(by Grandpa)

The ultimate story
  of God and Man,
act and consequence,
  what's God's plan—

Notice its totally
  honest tone—
it's about *this* life,
  not the unknown.

My God despises
  her ongoing depiction
as somehow condoning
  crucifixion.

275

A symbol of torture
   reaps applause?
The cross just naturally
   grew claws.

276

Could tossing that cross
   and dumping that cup
be a foolproof way
   to lighten up?

277

Saying these things
   is breaking rules?
Hey, we poets
   are licensed fools!

278

You'll get killed for joking
   about Mohammed—
and I had such a good one for you—
   dammit!

279

Green Grow the Rushdies, O

I had a tip
   (it's just a rumor)
that God's okayed
   a sense of humor.

280

Mutilation's a horror
    for sadists to relish;
going by the book
    can be pretty hellish.

281

For theft they chop off
    a foot or a hand—
if the theft is small enough,
    understand.

282

Perversion

If you're a woman,
    don't you dare
to tempt a man
    by showing hair.

Your nature's evil—
    big man's nature
better—backed
    by musculature.

Alcohol
    has been disowned,
but lying males
    can get you stoned.

283

Godspeak

To mutilate, torture,
*   is my decree?*
Revisit the Prophets,
*   they speak for me.*

284

I've got an in
    with the sublime—
my God can beat yours
    anytime.

We had a shooting
on our street,
a man went berserk
in the heat.

Grandpa pondered,
"We travel blind
when we seek to enter
another's mind.

"Childhood traumas,
current woes,
sometimes meld
and the center goes.

"Or life was blighted
before its call
by the hard-sell doom
of alcohol.

"Or mind-blotting agents
were present now—
but isn't that
someone's cash cow?

"Combined with evil
hyped on the screen,
profits paramount,
mean, obscene—

"Or perhaps sometimes—
but I'm no medic—
the cause could be
inborn, genetic.

"One gene the more,
    one gene the less,
I too could break
    beneath distress.

"Or maybe the cause
    would be lost in tears
if life progressed
    for a million years.

"But the deeper we delve
    the more we pause—
we know effects
    do have a cause.

"Which is not to deny
    the mind is free,
but just to rule out
    certainty.

"The fast one must stoop
    to empower the slow one;
everyone stands
    in the shadow of no one."

286

My Grandpa says,
    "I've seen a lot
of my fellow man,
    and given it thought;

"And here's the result—
    my credo, my Bible:
as soon as you label,
    you're guilty of libel."

287

I asked my Grandpa—
    not much tact—
if he were younger,
    how he'd act.

"Sometimes it's wise
    to push and go,
but for the most,
    I'd take it slow.

"I'd look ahead
    before I'd dash on,
and put a 'com'
    before my passion.

"I'd speak with forethought
    of even the 'worst' one:
condemning the act,
    but never the person."

288

"Enlightened self-interest—
    that's the key
to a world where most
    are safe and free.

"We must cherish all
    in our human relations,
since we live up or down
    to expectations.

"And 'cherish all'
    has another dimension,
which more and more urgently
    claims our attention."

The Doll syndrome

Rumor and Gossip
　　sit side by side
in a black stretch limo
　　marqued "De Ride".

Grandpa says, "Learning
　　what tongues can do
is easy: read Henry the Fourth,
　　Part Two."

Motive musing
(reflections on the unconscious)
(by Grandpa)

We're sitting in
    a subway train—
it seems to move,
    but look again—

It's the train beside it
    that's moving. We're
still sitting stationary
    here.

Is it like that with
    the way we see
the "whys" of our
    activity?

Is our sense of our
    true motives slack?
Do we fail to note
    another track?

Do we tend to clothe
    in Sunday best
what's really just
    self-interest?

Which is not to say
    we'd switch our grooving,
but it's nice to know
    which train is moving.

291

Our neighbor is retired now,
    he's got a lot of time
to do the things he couldn't do
    when he was in his prime.

But now he's "past it", so he says,
    "I now won't *do*, I'll talk;
I'll just sit in my mocking chair
    and mock around the clock."

292

The Neighbor's Reverie

In reminiscence,
    how they glow—
those golden chances
    long ago.

Nothing urgent
    in their voice,
they left you free
    to make your choice.

Was destiny singing
    her siren song?
What seems so right
    is often wrong.

The tide comes in,
    the tide goes out—
it's a voyage of dreams
    on a sea of doubt.

Uncle Lee suffered
    a heart attack,
but he recovered
    and came right back.
Now he preaches to everyone
    we should be
touching base with our
    mortality.
But Dad isn't buying;
    he cries, "Dagnab it!
that Lee is becoming
    a preacher of habit!"
And Mom adds, "By preaching
    most every place *we* go,
I fear he's developed
    an altar ego."

Uncle Lee claims
    he suffers detractions,
but Auntie Vi
    defends her actions:
"If I let him orate
    all day, he would;
he's got too much to say
    for my own good."

295

"The Ancient Mariner
        preached in Britain;
'He stoppeth one of three',
        it's written.

"But he wasn't a patch
        on your Uncle Lee;
that man stoppeth
        three of three."

296

"He speaks his mind,
        that I'll allow—
what there is of it,
        anyhow."

297

"Lee's kind of slow
        for the human race,
but his ego gallops
        at a goodly pace."

298

"My husband Lee,
        I fear, is very—
must I say it?—
        ordinary.

"That doesn't quite
        describe what Lee is—
extra ordinary
        he is."

299

"Though Lee is basically
     dense,
at times he seems
     to make some sense.

"He is, when all
     is said and done,
a complicated
     simpleton."

300

Auntie Vi
     says Uncle Lee
was once as handsome
     as could be.

"In one fell swoop—
     I find this galling—
he went from Apollo
     to appalling."

301

Uncle Lee declared,
     "Vi set her hooks,
and I married her
     because of her looks—

"But not the kind,
     I must avow,
that you can see
     I'm getting now."

302

"A whirlwind romance—
    it was all a blur—
I felt transported—
    (now I wish I were)."

303

"I know I have faults—
    that's one right there—
I have criticisms
    of me to spare.

"My own worst enemy's
    me, I've reckoned,
but Vi clocks in
    at a real close second."

304

Uncle Lee says,
    "I can't abide
her constant talk
    of my 'shadow side'.

"I've got one, I know,
    I'm of human stock,
and it's most pronounced
    at five o'clock."

Auntie Vi was attacking,
    Uncle Lee was cringing,
unable to stymie
    her verbal singeing:
"When I'm done you can talk
    till your eyelids sag,
but don't interrupt me
    when I'm in mid-nag."

Uncle Lee
    was doing some bragging
during a respite
    from Aunt Vi's nagging.

He thought she was busy
    in the other room,
but she opened the door
    like the clap of doom.

She called him a failure
    to his face;
it was, he said later,
    the coup de disgrace.

Uncle Lee said, "Vi's a Nagging U grad",
    but Auntie Vi gave tit for tat:
"Lee is nothing if not smart,
    and he isn't smart, I can vouch for that."

308

They were playing cards—
    Dad was running amuck,
and Mom was decrying
    the gods of bad luck.

But Uncle Lee cautioned,
    "Go easy, doll;
If it weren't for bad luck
    I'd have no luck at all."

309

"I sympathize
    with Vi's condition—
a very nagative
    disposition."

310

"If life's a novel—
    a hopefully long one—
I sometimes feel
    I got into the wrong one.

"'Turn a new leaf'
    is just a scam—
I turn the leaf
    and there I am."

311

"I feel I'm racing
    down life's freeway
and being given
    little Lee-way."

312

Aunt Vi upbraided
    Uncle Lee,
"The nerve—exchanging
    words with me!"

"I'm not exchanging words",
    he muttered,
"I stick with every one
    I've uttered."

313

Uncle Sid
    urged Uncle Lee
to stand up to his wife
    like a man born free.
Uncle Lee answered,
    "I'm normally pliable,
but this advice
    is just not Vi-able."

314

Whale of a bicker

Uncle Sid said,
    "It goes on and on—
I call it the
    Lee/Vi-athon."

315

Uncle Lee
    points to the screen,
and says, "See, Vi?
    It's gross, obscene."
She answers, "So?
    You want them banning?
Grow up, and stop
    your Peter Panning."

316

Uncle Lee said,
    "For what it's worth,
I feel that I'm
    the salt of the earth."

Aunt Vi answered,
    "Oh, be quiet;
I happen to be
    on a salt-free diet."

317

Brief encounter
(by Uncle Lee)

I left my briefcase
    by the door,
and she stepped on it
    as it hit the floor.

It did me good
    to see her face
when I righteously snarled,
    "Get off my case!"

318

"I give only suggestions,
    never orders;
I'm not one", said Aunt Vi,
    "of those overlorders.

"That being said,
    I admit there's no doubt
I insist my suggestions
    be carried out."

319

My Auntie Vi
    told my Uncle Sid,
"You'd better think twice
    and retract your bid."

They were playing cards,
    as you may have guessed,
and Uncle Lee
    was a bit distressed.

But Uncle Sid soothed,
    "She's only jokin';
your little Vi
    is a mite outspoken."

But Uncle Lee
    was a picture of gloom;
he dejectedly asked,
    "Outspoken by whom?"

320

"Shakespeare saw ages
    of man galore—
I think it was seven—
    I see four."

Uncle Lee paused:
    "First off, he's carried;
then married and harried,
    and finally, buried."

321

Uncle Lee
    acquired a dog,
"Alacrity",
    with whom to jog.

"And not only jog",
    said Uncle Lee,
"I do everything with
    Alacrity."

322

He's happy with
    his dog in tow,
but sighs he's never
    scooped so low.

323

Alacrity
    is glad to share
with Aunt Vi's haughty cat
    Pierre.

Pierre reciprocates,
    and he
enjoys a pounce
    on Uncle Lee.

But Uncle Lee
    accounts this scary;
he mutters "Harmless?
    Necessary?"

324

Pierre was basking;
    to bug his wife,
Uncle Lee upbraided him,
    "Get a life!"

Aunt Vi shot back,
    "*You're* one to brag?
You sail the Good Ship
    Lollygag."

When my cousin Cliff
    asked my Auntie Vi
how old she was,
    he got this reply:

"I'm as old as anyone's
    ever been
who can swim the ocean
    from rim to rim;

"Jump on a horse
    and traverse the land
from Kapuskasing
    to Samarkand;

"And plummet down
    from outer space
in a parachute
    of Chantilly lace.

"Staying youthful
    is all the rage,
but I'm never shy
    about giving my age."

"I don't really ride horses,
    I'm not an equestrian,
I don't even drive,
    I'm very pedestrian."

327

When I asked Aunt Vi
    how she liked my verse,
she paused, then said,
    "It could be worse—
maybe a little
    too namby-pambied—
but wait—do you want this
    candid or candied?"

328

"But I'm glad you enjoy
    being bouncy and Byrony;
it's a harmless exercise,
    pumping irony."

329

So what if she thinks
    my verses pallid?
My poetic license
    is no less valid.

Though rhyme and rhythm
    are deemed a sin,
and obfuscation's
    clearly in,

I can still aspire
    to share the stage
with the murky riders
    of the purple page.

No readers, but . . .

Bestowing awards
in incestuous sessions,
these poets are truly
our most prized possessions.

In good company
(by Grandpa)

Awards? The ones
deserving most
are often standing
at the post.

Invisible,
anonymous,
'Shakespeare', 'Homer',
missed the bus.

They stand as surrogates
for all
who get the curse
and not the call.

Progress

Our modern poets
lard galore
with image, symbol,
metaphor.

By contrast, Homer's
spare and tight;
our bards could teach him
how to write!

333

Ah well, I've got
    no cause for cursin'—
our modern bard's
    a navel person—

And weaving sails
    of belly lint,
he's off on seas
    of whine-dark print.

334

It's simple, why this "poetry"'s divined
    as worthless: it ignores (in Byronese)
"The gentle reader, who may wax unkind,
    And, caring little for the author's ease,
Insist on knowing what he means, a hard
And hapless situation for a bard."

335

As a poet I'm not a pro,
    for sure;
I'm just a rankling
    amateur.

336

Van Gogh made zilch
    in the painting biz;
will *my* fate be
    the same as his?

I picked up a card
    that may signal so:
"Go direct to jail.
    Do not pass Van Gogh."

337

Since the fates are notorious
    for the ways they can flimflam us,
might I wake up one morning
    and find myself infamous?

338

Uncle Sid's married
    to Auntie Nana—
she's famous for being
    a Pollyanna.

He said, "Don't mistake me,
    it's not that I'm whining,
but all the refiners
    are busy refining,

The mills are all milling,
    the miners all mining,
to keep her supplied
    with silver lining."

Uncle Lee answered,
    "Take Vi instead;
all *her* linings
    are certified lead."

339

Uncle Sid said,
    "In crises and fits,
I've frequently had to
    gather my wits.

"I may have missed some,
    but I'm sure—don't laugh—
I'm in possession
    at least of half."

But Aunt Nana wasn't
    amused a bit;
she said he was straining
    at the wit.

340

The Joker's Paradox

Uncle Sid says,
    "I've always defied
the law of 'gravity'
    (or at least I've tried).

"That's the only way
    I've ever found
to be sure both feet
    stay on the ground.

"So I'm never startled
    when I'm told
that levity's worth
    its weight in gold."

"In most situations
    of sorrow and pain,
the humorist goes for
    the jocular vein.

"Is doing this easy?
    The answer is no;
the humorist has a
    hard row to ho-ho."

Ha
(by Uncle Sid)

I tell a joke,
    and when I'm done,
well—half a laugh
    is better than none.

Serious business
(by Uncle Sid)

Though repeating the fact
    may tend to weary us,
the jolliest star in the sky
    is Sirius.

The implications
    are astronomic;
the cosmic validates
    the comic.

344

"A lot of humor
　　is much too labored;
it's sparkling lightness
　　that's sought and savored.

"It would probably further
　　the cause of gaiety
to run some courses
　　in spontaneity."

345

"At a recent meeting
　　that was somewhat strained,
I was asked what thoughts
　　I entertained.

"I answered, 'Madam,
　　in no degree
do I entertain thoughts;
　　they entertain me.'"

346

My cousin Danny
　　was one year old,
and I watched his birthday
　　bash unfold.

A discussion arose
　　as to who the tyke,
giggling and gurgling,
　　looked most like.

Aunt Debby opined,
　　"Churchill, by far."
Uncle Sid: "Close,
　　but no cigar."

347

Aunt Nana is known
    for her sumptuous cooking;
Uncle Sid says
    he requires a booking.

"Everyone scarfs here,
    it's hard to get seatin';
that is the snake
    in this Garden of Eatin'."

348

My sister Sue
    gets somewhat miffed
at these fleshy feasts,
    if you get my drift.

She once left the table
    with this dissent:
"Eat away, folks,
    to your hearts' discontent."

349

Sue says our appetite's
    what dooms us;
"The flesh we eat
    in turn consumes us.

"Of all foods speeding
    our demise,
the big bad HARMburger
    takes the prize."

350

"Despite its health-
    related toll,
the hot dog's clearly
    on a roll."

351

"A steak with fries
    will make you pay;
it's a hearty meal
    in a hurty way."

352

"You might ask yourself,
    Is it really smart
to drive a steak
    right through your heart?"

353

You Gotta Have Heart
(by Sue)

A heart has just so many ticks
    within it,
and it's ticking away there
    every minute.
If it's all ticked out
    before it's due,
I'd be really ticked off
    and so will you.

354

"We make new hearts
in the factory;
they come with a lifetime
guarantee."

355

"Meat wrecks the body,
but I'll not
deny it offers
food for thought."

356

Six billion sold out
(by Sue)

With the rainforests gone
we'll have lost the battle
in a drama entitled
"Revenge of the Cattle".

Our tombstone will be
a golden calf,
and golden arches
our cenotaph.

357

"The Meat Producers
held their ball
(an annual thing)
in Montreal.

"They danced and feasted,
then took a break
before the crowning
of their 'Miss Steak'."

358

"The elegant diner
    stuffs fois gras—
that tortured liver—
    down his maw.

"He's bursting with pride
    in his fawned-on station—
the very acme
    of civilization."

359

"At Oxford dinners
    the faculty grapple
with a whole roast pig,
    complete with apple.

"The erudite talk
    makes a merry din:
philosophy, morals,
    how crispy the skin."

360

Hot cuisine
(by Sue)

In Tokyo
    the new Four Seasons
is *the* hotel
    for many reasons.

But one is the world-class
    teppan grill—
a bit on the pricey side,
    but still—

When they hit that grill
    the shrimp are flapping—
so fresh! so fresh!
    The diners, clapping,

Drink to their loved ones
    with sparkling eyes.—
You say this is hell,
    not paradise?

361

"Seoul food (that's puppy
    on a tray)—
snakes skinned alive
    in old Taipei—

"Frogs' legs, of course,
    (the squirming, flopping
rest thrown on a heap
    of sopping

"Bloody flesh)—
    Bon appétit!
We're master chefs
    of agony."

"It's not my goal
　　to make you freak—
I speak for those
　　who cannot speak—
but *feel* as much
　　as you and I,
or more; we feel so little.
　　Why?"

Impotent rage
(by Sue)

Animal parts
　　are the hellish credo
of millions of men
　　with low libido.

These malefactors
　　trade devastation
for stand-up comic
　　hallucination—

Mandating a planet
　　of smoldering embers
to harmonize
　　with their burnt-out members.

"Species at risk
　　for this stunned brood?
The world's in penile
　　servitude."

365

"Tiger, tiger, burning bright
in the forests of the night,
what amoral hand and eye
dare choke your flame and watch it die?"

366

Metaphor War
(by Sue)

Your carcass-chomping
    dude tut-tuts
that vegetarians
    are nuts.

Sometimes his view
    becomes more grim—
those fruitcakes better
    not bug *him*.

The thought of meat-deprived
    mañanas
drives him (as he would say)
    bananas.

I, on the other hand,
    eschew
his fare—it renders him
    ragout.

And that's at best—
    I can recall
some going stark sirloin,
    up the wall.

I must report
    on some men, sadly:
they have been wienerschnitzelled,
    badly.

Survival of the Unfattest
(by Sue)

"Guns or butter",
    they used to say,
to draw a line
    'twixt night and day.

But those are no longer
    the words we utter;
we know there's death
    in guns *and* butter.

"We enjoy the Earth's surface,
    not lying beneath,
but we're getting there fast
    by the sin of our teeth."

Amazing Grain
(by Sue)

Amazing grain, how sweet the smell
    of veggies with brown rice!
Buckwheat I dote upon as well,
    and barley too is nice.

If you are battered to your knees
    (and buttered, speaking plain),
you'll clear your clogged-up arteries
    with this amazing grain.

Amazing grain, amazing grain,
    it saved a wretch like me,
and yet it's looked on with disdain,
    because it's almost free.

Amazing grain, how blest this place
    of soil and sun and rain!
Sing out the praise of Earth, and grace
    that manifests in grain.

Cornucopia
(by Sue)

Carrot and radish
    and lush snow pea,
sweet potato
    and broccoli,
mango, pistachio,
    strawberry—
Lord, what foods
    these morsels be!

Godspeak

I've given you food
in a festive flood—
what more do you want, my children?
Blood?

It's a caution
(by Sue)

Immunity:
    it's hard to beat;
when sugared less
    life can be sweet.

      * * *

Blood pressure high?
    Could be *your* fault;
spare yourself
    that salt assault.

      * * *

Protect yourself
    from too much sun;
be known as a
    reflective one.

      * * *

Beefsteak tomatoes
    are a treat,
and closest we should come
    to meat.

      * * *

The rule of gold:
    Don't be surprised
if healthful truths
    aren't advertised.

373

Balancing budgets
(by Sue)

Try to imagine
　　what a sum
we'll save when the
　　curriculum

Requires 'Wellness'
　　for its passes—
in schools and even
　　medic classes.

374

Co-captains of our fate?
(by Grandpa)

"Old age is a shipwreck"—
　　Need it be?
We can't outwit
　　mortality—

But perhaps read weather,
　　tack and thwart,
and sail it gently
　　into port.

375

"Are we ready for old age?
　　In no wise;
even winter catches us
　　by surprise."

376

Fast-food update

Nothing beats a
gooey pizza,
and I get real edgy
for a burger (veggie).
Pasta is lagging,
but soon (I'm funning)
fasta pasta
will be off and running.

377

I was hungry and gazed
    at the summer sky—
the big full moon
    was a lemon pie
in a sea of meringue—
    I was quite surprised:
"Pie in the sky"
    had materialized.

My Grandpa likes
    to prune and hoe,
and watch the things
    he planted grow.

"It's all a mystery,
    my boy;
accept, be humble,
    and enjoy.

"The wisest man,
    though probing deep,
soon or later
    goes to sleep.

"He takes up but
    a little room,
and helps the lovely
    flowers bloom."

"Topsoil," says Grandpa,
    "gets in your blood;
the greatest miracle
    lies in mud.

"Minutely it builds up
    day by day—
regeneration
    out of decay.

"Ants and beetles
    labor and hum,
and the final blessing—
    the earthworms come.

"Then, we humans
    get to play with it,
after the worms
    have had their way with it."

380

Uncle Sam
    teaches English Lit,
and he likes my book,
    what he's seen of it.

But he says its potential
    is hard to gauge:
"It's a little bit tame
    for this day and rage."

381

Uncle Sam lives
     at a pretty fast pace;
he says fast living
     is no disgrace.

"The only sin
     is being bored;
lack of virtue
     is its own reward."

382

Uncle Sam calls himself
     "Basic Sam"—
"I'm a child of the earth;
     I am what I am.

"I have no use
     for obscure speculation;
it's only a form
     of social sedation.

"Man doesn't live
     by the loony ethereal;
the spirit, my boy,
     is immaterial."

383

"My object:
     to cavort in life;
not the spartan life,
     but the sportin' life."

384

"There's lots of time,
    when it's too late
to celebrate,
    to cerebrate."

385

"When I see the blood
    in religion's mist,
I thank God I'm
    an atheist."

386

Invisible Love
(by Grandpa)

The atheist,
    it seems to me,
is the crowning work
    of the Deity,
for "you all know
    security
is mortals' chiefest
    enemy."

387

Uncle Sam wrote
    a "defective" novel;
he says he likes it
    and will not grovel.

"If you let them see
    you're prone to give-ins,
they'll cut your manuscript
    to ribbons.

"You've got to compromise,
    it's true,
but you draw the line
    when they throw out *you*.

"But every animal
    has its predator,
and every writer
    has his editor."

388

"My book will be
    an instant hit:
The Sunrise I've
    entitled it.

"It's what we know,
    from standard lore,
the whole world has
    been waiting for."

389

"I set a limit
   on my next book's length
(I consider terseness
   my greatest strength).

"I thought I'd be finished
   by yesterday noon,
but I sailed through my limit
   like a hot-air balloon."

390

"Writing novels
   I like the best—
I can give the footnote thing
   a rest.

"Bullfrogs chorus
   'ribbid, ribbid',
and academics
   'ibid, ibid'."

Psychobabble Blues
(by Uncle Sam)

I'm not a prude,
>   but I put my foot down
at "anal-retentive",
>   that silly put-down.

The fellow who coined it
>   was some kind of dope;
we're all retentive that way,
>   I hope.

I wouldn't want any
>   (I'm sure you'll agree)
but anal-retentive folk
>   visiting *me*.

Foundering vessels
(by Uncle Sam)

High on my roster
    of condemnings
are publishers,
    those lurid lemmings.

The Bible would have
    been dismissed
by most of them:
    "Won't fit our list."

But give them some
    sadistic murder,
they'll underwrite
    a million-worder.

In tribute to
    great books they've bounced,
let's hope their "lists"
    get more pronounced.

393

"They call themselves 'publishers'?
    Take a hike!
'Rubbishers'
    would be more like."

394

"There *is* the odd good one,
    old and new;
my canvas is wide,
    so my brush is too."

395

Small mercies
(by Uncle Sam)

The genre's swamping us,
    so please,
no more murder
    mysteries.

Do you think some day
    we might advance
to *wounding* mysteries,
    perchance?

396

Hey, get with it
(by Uncle Sam)

There's a Retcher Scale
    for heinous crime—
let's say a penny
    to a dime—
if it scores a six
    or more for slime,
the bucks will be big,
    the slotting prime,
which is why the media
    have no time
for "anal-retentive"
    guys like I'm.

397

"Their knowledge of human nature
        stops
at sex, perversion, murder,
        cops.
In their own perception their product's
        tops,
on a human scale they churn out
        flops."

398

Who needs them?
(by Uncle Sam)

Literary
        agents, too,
belong in some
        jurassic zoo.
They'll preen to mate
        bombastic brutes,
but to the humble
        hoist their snoots.

You wish
(by Uncle Sam)

A writer was proudly
    heard to say
his characters "took off",
    "got away";
what he really hoped was—
    if I may—
they weren't mere cardboard,
    but papier-mâché.
(This modest wish
    proved *très outré*—
they vanished like
    a wisp of spray.)

All too true disclaimer
(by Uncle Sam)

"My characters bear",
    the writer said,
"resemblance to no one
    living or dead."
His artistic achievements
    may be slight,
but let's be fair:
    he got *that* right.

Uncle Sam: "Movies
today are rot;
most of those movies
shouldn't be shot.
(They reek,
historically.)"

Uncle Sid: "Maybe
I misunderstood;
you said that they *shouldn't*?
They certainly *should*.
(I speak
metaphorically.)"

402

Steroid but sterile
(by Uncle Sam)

Surface hysterics, with
dearth at the core,
give new meaning to
"crashing bore".

403

"They're confident
they can really slay 'em
under the banner
of General Mayhem."

404

"Imbecile sex,
     blood, and sound
all fuzzed, to make it
     seem profound . . .

"Tumble, Rumble,
     Mumble, is
the Holy Trinity
     of filmbiz."

405

"The odd good movie
     still gets made,
an aberration
     in the trade.

"You wonder how
     they could have missed 'em?
There's no such thing
     as a perfect system."

Hardcore Lament

"When it comes to hardcore,"
    said Uncle Sam,
"every person
    should give a damn.

"We tend to mimic
    the things we see,
and I don't want mimicking
    done on *me*.

"My colleagues cut me up
    like a peach,
but it's nice to keep it
    a figure of speech.

"So it seems to me
    that the rest of our trip
should perhaps be taken
    by censor-ship."

"*Ex*pression / *re*pression,
    that's not the issue;
the only thing here is
    protection of tissue."

Guess
(by Uncle Sam)

The arts today
    overflow our cup—
Have the floodgates opened
    or the sewers backed up?

40.9

"Speaking of life's
    artistic wrongs,
every sapseeper
    now writes songs.

"But there's no percentage
    in our rebuking,
since babies *will* be
    mewling and puking."

410

"Avoiding the spray
    from their ears as they leap,
we'll learn all about life
    from our little bo creep."

411

Ode to Bo Creep
(by Uncle Sam)

You've discovered sex,
    but you're such a bore—
it's all been said
    and done before—

And so incredibly
    better, too—
though the end result
    was tragic: *you.*

412

"One thing about
    these geeky guys—
they're impossible
    to satirize."

Storming Parnassus
(by Uncle Sam)

In Roman days
    the entertaining
was gripping fare,
    if somewhat draining.

Blood flowed like vino
    from a vat,
while maned performers
    chewed the fat,

And gave the world
    unique instruction
on staging a
    bare-bones production.

A churchly Europe
    next awoke
in times when artists
    went baroque.

Audiences,
    posh and tatty,
trooped in droves
    to hear castrati,

And whooped, as roles
    were brought to life
by male sopranos,
    "Hail the knife!"

Our modern age,
    though still outclassed,
is trying hard
    to match the past,

And going by recent
    sounds and sights,
seems certain to
    surpass those heights.

414

"We've empowered a hatch
    of puffed-up babies
to inflict a plague
    of artistic rabies.

"Society should have
    had the gumption
to label, 'Not fit
    for adult consumption.'"

415

Enterpainment
(by Uncle Sam)

I've pondered how
    the system works,
concluding that
    it favors jerks—

And I contend
    this answer is
a reasoned, fair
    analysis.

"Nudity can be
    rear or frontal,
but best is full,
    and horizontal.

"This predilection
    isn't lewd;
I just like sleeping
    in the nude."

Goodbye Columbus

My Uncle Sam
    is on sabbatical,
and has time to indulge
    his bent for the radical.

Distortion of history
    gets him hot:
"Something's at work—
    I won't say what—

"But the eyewitness annals
    that might well numb us
are all but ignored
    in the case of Columbus.

"The official record
    by de las Casas
says forty million
    lads and lasses,

"Parents and grandparents,
    old and young,
were starved, dismembered,
    burned and hung.

"But somewhere at work
    are revisionist elves—
it's all disappeared
    from the library shelves.

"Of course, truth will triumph—
    they're not that clever—
they can't suppress
    the truth forever.

"You can only construct—
    this is no surprise—
a house of cards
    from a pack of lies."

418

"Should all those 'Columbias'
    change their name?
Of course—they're bearing
    a mark of shame.

"Russia courageously
    shucked the bad,
even the matchless
    Stalingrad.

"The sine qua non
    of respectable entity:
claiming the right
    to a clear identity."

419

Uncle Sam says,
    "If you study the past,
nothing much changes
    except the cast.

"We hit a dead end
    through our own behavior,
and the first thing you know
    we cry for a savior.

"For a while we're happy
    to have a master,
but of course he leads us
    to disaster.

"The same thing happens
    again and again,
but we never learn;
    we're like sheep from a pen.

"The herd seeks a hero
    to order and gate it;
'herd' and 'hero'
    are closely related."

420

"Looking for 'leaders'—
    what a crock!
I guess we look at ourselves
    and balk."

Media rare
(by Uncle Sam)

If only a few
    own the Press and TV,
does that put the "mock"
    in democracy?

Red light district
(by Uncle Sam)

We should pay close heed
    when the powerful few speak,
bearing in mind
    Orwellian Newspeak.

Do death squads foster
    "Democracy"?
Is degrading the Earth
    "Security"?

Money talks
    any way you stack it,
and owning the media,
    what a racket!

The Daily Smoke and Mirror
(by Uncle Sam)

They want to control us
　　with omissions, slant, jargon,
and they want us to pay for it
　　into the bargain.
Somebody tell me
　　why it's not
like digging your grave
　　before you're shot.

Mediaspeak
(by Uncle Sam)

It's good to have standards—
　　everyone should—
and double standards
　　are doubly good.

You don't have to stretch
　　your brains too far—
we'll tell you what
　　the issues are.

We're huge on sports
　　and the jilted lover—
we cover these
　　for the things we cover.

We're here to smokescreen
　　the Big Boys' theft—
we love it when branded
　　too far left.

Right thinking
(by Uncle Sam)

The effects of brainwashing
    being subliminal,
our perception of them
    is minimal—
any suspicions make *us*
    feel criminal.

Rogers redux
(by Uncle Sam)

The problem isn't
    what we don't know,
it's what we're sure of
    that just ain't so.

A corollary thought
    has some allure:
What we don't know guards
    what we know for sure.

"If slaveowners ran
    the system called 'slavery',
and feudal lords
    the feudal knavery,
then isn't it odd
    to think that *we*
run capitalism's
    'democracy'?"

Back on Planet Earth
(by Uncle Sam)

Does a Secret Council
  of oligarchs
meet to rule us,
    the dimwit marks?

Our elected leaders
    just a screen
behind which purrs
    the real machine?

These are questions
  of shattering force,
but the answer's a simple one:
    of course.

Ill fares the land . . .
(by Uncle Sam)

How dense is this
    oligarchal core?
'Sixty Families' once,
    now more—
(we're talking States here)—
    perhaps four score.
They choose the things
    you're against and for,
if you live or die,
    if it's peace or war.
Hey, *somebody* has to
    mind the store!

430

"'Droit du seigneur'
    was feudal practice—
we agree how evil
    such an act is—

"We've learned, in these
    enlightened days,
to do the deed
    in well-bred ways."

Nothing's sacred
(Charitable Gifts Act, *Ontario, 1949)*
(by Uncle Sam)

A town ill-Starred,
       and Globe and Maily,
at one time had
       a people's daily.

The owner died,
       and in his will
decreed it stay
       unneutered still,

And founded, to
       that worthy end,
a charitable trust.
       Perpend:

The Oligarchy,
       seeing red,
lashed out boldly
       at the dead,

And passed (the damnedest
       thing you saw)
a quashing
       retroactive law.

Of course, the deed
       is buried deep—
Ontario
       is still asleep—

And memory
       can never stir
with what the media
       inter.

At the Oligarchs' Ball
(by Uncle Sam)

"Here's to Free Markets!"
    (nudge nudge, wink wink),
"Free Press! Free Press!"
    (yuk yuk, clink clink).

Talk about NAFTA? Excuse our lafta.
(by Uncle Sam)

Our rulers' media
    blared 'Disgrace!'
when a judge banned news
    in a murder case.

They put on a loud
    democratic show
of the public's sacred
    right to know.

But when a protest
    march was planned,
designed to galvanize
    the land

On the meaning of NAFTA,
    a crucial issue,
they gave more space
    to Mogadishu.

In fact they gave
    no space at all
to this belated
    wake-up call,

Which nevertheless
    turned out to be
the biggest march
    in our history.

Now, *that* was *NEWS!*
    So they ran the tap
for murder, sports,
    "entertainment" pap.

But where's the beef?
    We have it good;
we've the right to know
    what they feel we should.

434

The Oligarchy
(by Uncle Sam)

They're hidden from
    the public view;
that's what their media
    can do.

Their politicians
    take the lumps—
they let them go
    from champs to chumps.

435

"They call it 'bowling':
    they take a clown,
they raise 'em up,
    then they knock 'em down—

"That way the anger
    is always directed
against some pinhead
    we've elected."

436

Poll-ution
(by Uncle Sam)

One way the System
    rock-and-rolls
is skillful use
    of phony polls.

They huff and puff
    their current goofus,
and then poll-vault them
    into office.

437

The Bandwagon Dragon
(by Uncle Sam)

"Get on the bandwagon,
    show you're willing!"—
The lying polls
    can be self-fulfilling.

438

Disraeli update
(by Uncle Sam)

Three kinds of lies
    assault our souls:
lies, damned lies,
    and polls.

439

"If a tiny group's
    going to wield dominion,
it *must* give the public
    its 'public opinion'."

440

"Is it hard finding shearers
    to shear the sheep?
Are the heavens high?
    Is the ocean deep?
Applicants aren't
    what the Oligarchs need—
their problem is how
    to control the stampede."

441

"But selection is still important:
    Why?
They want the best politicians
    that money can buy."

442

Rocky Mountin'
(by Uncle Sam)

"I wonder
    who's Kissinger
        now?"
No wonder,
    and no wonder
        how.

443

"Along with the shearing
    their job is to pull
a cap to our noses
    produced from *our* wool."

444

Election time
(by Uncle Sam)

Every four or five years
    there comes the great day
when the sheep are unpenned
    and permitted to play.

They baa their assent
    to whatever's been done,
and jounce back exulting
    "We won! We won!"

445

Jobs, Jobs, Jobs
(by Uncle Sam)

New drums a-beating—
    nice to hear
those sounds in our
    election year.

But soon we learn
    that new drums, old drums,
they are, in fact,
    the same old dole drums.

Mentioning no names . . .
(by Uncle Sam)

Though wide his scope
    and broad his bent,
a politician's
    up for rent.

He serves a cause
    until it's done
all it can do
    for Number One.

Cracking the Gracci
(by Uncle Sam)

Sometimes there'll be
    a people's pol
whose object's not
    to make a haul—

The System then
    will throw the book
and get them out
    by hook or crook.

448

Oh, Brother!
(by Uncle Sam)

I often yearn
    for days of yore—
even nineteen
    eighty-four.

It's true your phone
    could be "switched on"
to pick up every
    grunt and yawn.

But Big Bro had
    no eyes to *see*—
and now he does,
    through your TV.

He's out to totally
    enfold you
(but don't tell anyone
    I told you).

449

To Serve and Protect—guess who?
(by Uncle Sam)

Does all this surveillance
    make you less fitful?
Will you turn in your handgun,
    retire your pit bull?

I'm afraid *your* protection
    is not on the menu;
it isn't done *for* you,
    but mainly *agen* you.

205

Progress Report
(by Uncle Sam)

The big thief was praised,
    the little thief stomped—
that's the way it was
    when King Lear romped.

It's so different now
    you'd be amazed—
the little thief's stomped,
    the big thief's praised.

Progress Report II
(by Uncle Sam)

A ruling class
    of giant sharks,
a rich milieu
    of tasty marks . . .

Things *have* evolved—
    the game is vaster,
the sharks are bigger now
    and faster.

"... *the people perish*"
(by Uncle Sam)

There's no escape
     in the global village
from Corporate tyranny
     and pillage.

They want the world
     to be free, all right—
free for them
     to exploit and blight.

Business thinking
     can only bring
raw contempt
     for the vision thing.

Ship of Fools
(by Uncle Sam)

The seas we sail
 are pretty grim,
but the Oligarchy's
 in fighting trim.

Their hold is stocked,
 their decks secure
against the thrashings
 of the poor.

Do they care that the waters
 boil and seethe?
It's the very stuff
 of the air they breathe.

They feel that life
 would be rather dull
devoid of fingernails
 scratching the hull.

Thar she blows?
(by Uncle Sam)

"It's well in hand,
    no need to panic",
they soothed the steerage
    on *Titanic.*

Meanwhile they locked
    each stairwell gate
and put a double
    lock on fate.

A few grabbed implements
    to wreck
the barriers
    and reach the deck.

Have things much changed?
    Well, let me warn ya:
the standby ship's
    the *California.*

"The jails are full,
    you can be sure,
of people there
    because they're poor.

"If you're born with *two* strikes,
    take my word,
some judge may whistle in
    the third."

"Meanwhile the lawless,
    secret, fetid
oligarchal rule's
    abetted.

"It's an exercise
    from an old, old school—
the 'rule of law'
    is the law of rule."

World-class city
(by Uncle Sam)

The rich are stepping
    out to play;
no sleeping on
    the sidewalks, eh?

Revolutions
(by Uncle Sam)

When one percent
    own half the nation,
the stage is set
    for conflagration.

The spark can be
    tea, bread, or "cake"
(a dumb remark
    someone might make).

Will we ever learn?
    My guess is no;
around and around
    and around we go.

459

Patriotism
(by Uncle Sam)

"England expects . . . "
    read Nelson's flags,
then 'England' let his loved one
    die in rags.
,

"Ask not what your country . . . "
    Kennedy said,
and then his 'country'
    shot him dead.

460

"Prime Minister, Party,
    President,
they're really all
    irrelevant.

"They fill their designated
    slots,
but the Oligarchy
    calls the shots."

461

"When these big shots play
    they throw a mean ball—
first the brushback,
    then the beanball."

462

"There's a lot of ballistic
    evidence
for how logical is
    the hesitance
of the most well-meaning
    Presidents."

463

"Whenever a President's
        head is whacked,
you can rest assured
        it's a real class act."

464

"A President's head
        in the agent's sights
puts a certain spin
        on 'human rights'.

"We could all agree
        it's a bit abusive,
and the secret government's
        quite intrusive."

Taboo
(by Uncle Sam)

How many hundreds
    of others have died
to cover the tracks
    of presicide?

And how many thousands,
    in all, done in
within the walls
    of the "loony bin"?

Or simply pushed
    onto subway tracks
by authorized
    oligarchal hacks?

Or run off the road
    on fine clear days,
or died in other
    unprobed ways?

This is a story
    never told—
the life-and-death power
    plutocrats hold.

"Many strange 'suicide'
    deaths have occurred,
in circumstances
    bizarre and blurred.

"Monroe, Kilgallen,
    Reppert, Foster,
glow in the eerie
    midnight roster.

"The suspicious soul
    might be more lenient
if each such death
    were less convenient."

Pitiful Giant
(by Uncle Sam)

The most powerful man
    on this spinning sphere
is really the weakest,
    gnawed by fear.

Every word
    that he whispers or barks
is relayed at once
    to the Oligarchs.

They play a cruel
    psycho game
to keep him guessing,
    confused, hurt . . . tame.

The Secret Service
    guards him well—
there's no escaping
    from its shell.

Only the shower,
    when on full force,
may offer a venue
    for free discourse.

So there you have it:
    the People's Choice
stripped of focus,
    decision, voice.

468

Plutocraspeak
(by Uncle Sam)

Though the people vote,
    a White House resident
answers to *us*
    like a good little President.

We won't brook a President
    who rebels;
he'll do what he's told to do,
    or else.

469

"The hidden reach
    is long and sinister—
Chilean President,
    Swedish Prime Minister—

"Freely elected,
    they pose a threat—
step out of line,
    knocked off, no sweat."

470

Convergence
(by Uncle Sam)

"How long are you going
    to go on killing?"
Stalin was asked.
    His reply was chilling:

"As long as it's necessary."
    Ugh.
But some would knowingly smile,
    and shrug.

Late, but . . .
(by Uncle Sam)

Kudos to President
    Eisenhower,
who knew the truth
    and didn't cower.

They'd be curtailed
    in abuse of power
if more spoke up
    like Eisenhower.

472

"But the speaking up
    must be confident, clear—
they have nothing to fear
    but the lack of fear."

473

"I think you'll agree
    it's about high time
we all got involved
    in fighting crime."

474

USA Today
(by Uncle Sam)

Home of the brave?
    With explanation:
you'll find him on
    the reservation.

Kick him again, he's still twitching
(by Uncle Sam)

The Yankee Oligarchy's
    law:
you can never stuff too much
    in your craw.

Negotiating
    in peace or war,
they always break
    a deal—for more.

Their attitude:
    should a man concede,
that shows he's weak—
    now make him bleed.

We've got the power,
    give him a sample—
when you've got him down,
    make an example.

No deeper vision
    guides their fight;
these sharks are just
    pure appetite.

They're the enemy of
    humanity,
and we must understand
    our enemy.

476

We'll Rock ya, feller,
We'll Harry you, man
(or, Speaking of terrorists . . .)
(by Uncle Sam)

Latin Americans
    daily feel
Chiquita Banana's
    sharp-edged steal.

The death-squads torture
    before they kill—
orders from Bro,
    who foots the bill.

Lips razored out,
    eyes gouged—what fare
to add to the feast
    in Delaware.

Hidden, of course,
    behind thick veils
of "human rights"
    and other tales.

477

Old Gory
(by Uncle Sam)

Horrors unequalled
    in the annals of war—
Nam, Guatemala,
    El Salvador.

Stars for agony,
    torture's stripes—
fit flag for cruel
    rockpont types.

Say Uncle
(by Uncle Sam)

What unbridled savagery,
   hell and horror,
to establish the human
   pecking order!

Who's to stop us?
(by Uncle Sam)

The World Court's judgment
   that Managua,
not Washington,
   rules Nicaragua

Was garbage to
   the rockpont eagle,
that knows no legal
   or illegal.

It contra-vened
   the Court's decree,
and ripped its prey
   more cruelly.

Monroe Rockgrin
(by UncleSam)

Whenever you're feeling
   democracy's tug,
Big Bro's boot
   will squash you like a bug.

Secrets of hell
(by Uncle Sam)

We've heard of Dachau
    as a rule,
but not Fort Benning,
    the torture school.

That's where outward
    humans drill
in ways to mutilate
    to kill.

Tongues, eyeballs, are
    certificates
of the denatured
    graduates.

The world's most evil
    place; I find
I can't get Georgia
    off my mind.

"Georgia's a highly
    moral state—
you can land in jail
    if you fornicate.

"They'll soon let you know
    you don't belong
if you can't distinguish
    right from wrong."

The Rocky Horror Real Life Show
(by Uncle Sam)

When little kids just three years old
    are hung by CIA,
their parents' faces then carved up
    before they're blown away—

And other kids barbed-wire raked
    (their parents forced to watch)
until their bones are bare of flesh,
    while rockpont's sipping scotch—

These never-topped atrocities
    may echo down the eons,
but *we* don't give a goddam, do we?
    Hell, they're only peons.

Media blackout
(by Uncle Sam)

You've not seen a word of this,
    I expect;
it's not the news
    that they select;
it's not politically
    correct.

485

The Gacy gambit, big-time
(by Uncle Sam)

Old rockpont bro
    is quite the little actor—
he bills himself
    as a "benefactor".

What kind of response
    would perfectly suit?
I think a barrage
    of blood-soaked fruit.

486

Onward and Downward
(by Uncle Sam)

Hanging women
    by the ankles,
breasts sliced off,
    somehow rankles.

Skin peeled back
    from the face,
tongue cut out—
    a disgrace.

Couldn't rockpont
    be beguiled
to merely crucify?
    Nah, too mild.

The hairy man,
    the rockpont ghoul—
they set high standards
    in their school.

487

Apology to Central America
*(by Uncle Sam, with a little help
from a friend)*

O pardon me,
you bleeding piece of Earth,
that I am meek and gentle with
these butchers.

488

Evil Empire
(appearance / reality 101)
(by Uncle Sam)

Tortured fiefdoms,
    their baronial
slavers self-billed
    "anti-colonial".

Steel boots stomping
    from the heights,
foul mouth screeching
    "human rights".

The iron fists
    rest cozily
in mittens stitched
    "democracy".

Kafka, Orwell,
    seers of power,
this would be
    your finest hour!

489

Who's Tory now?
(by Uncle Sam)

Nam's people rose
    from the colony mat;
rockpont bro said
    We can't have *that.*

490

"By smashing Cambodia's
    peaceful realm
they let Pol Pot
    usurp the helm.

"He killed a million or two,
    so what?
They still secretively
    bet the Pot."

491

The Information Society
(by Uncle Sam)

Take a peek,
    if you want to see more,
at Indonesia,
    and East Timor.

But even a peek
    is hard to get,
and every day
    gets harder yet.

A few small mags,
    and after that
I guess we go
    to samizdat.

492

Exclusive: Bro explains East Timor genocide
(by Uncle Sam)

"Why do we smash
a chickenshit state
through our Indonesian
surrogate?

"First off, they're only
a bunch of gooks;
they're lucky we don't
unleash our nukes.

"But mostly, a warning
to never coddle
rebels who opt
for another model.

"We want conformity,
not fuss;
we want the whole world
Timorous."

493

Uh-oh
(by Uncle Sam)

Clark Airforce Base—
the power and dash of it!
But Pinatubo
made an ash of it.

Right on the money
(People power vs. Superpower)
(by Uncle Sam)

There's a way to bring justice
    into play—
a worldwide boycott
    night and day
of everything linked
    to the U.S.A.

This is the price
    they'll have to pay
for a few blood families
    holding sway.

"Where do we start?
    What do we chop?
Pop 'em in the snoot
    with unsold pop."

Universal Tea Party
(by Uncle Sam)

There were stirrings of true
    democracy
when Americans totalled
    a shipment of tea.

What's needed now—
    spurning "good buys"—
is more tea totallers
    like those guys.

"Advertising
    is the siren song
the sly blood families
    ride along.

"Resisting it
    won't be a trial
when you see the power
    in your denial."

498

For whom the bell tolls
(by Uncle Sam)

The Armada mass
    of the rockpont eagle
has been outsailed
    by the Cuban seagull.

Invasion, embargo,
    assassination,
she somehow eludes
    the planned predation.

Billions for poisons,
    provocateurs,
she endured it all,
    and still endures.

Whatever the outcome
    on this spit of time,
Cuba foreshadows
    the monster's decline.

Natural Law
(by Uncle Sam)

The pressure builds
    along the fault—
the symmetry
    of vile assault.

To torture, murder,
    seems a cinch,
but wise men know
    there's no free lynch.

And crown thy good . . .
(the death of Jim Crow)
(by Uncle Sam)

Before it became
    a travesty,
Rock 'n' Roll
    set America "free".

Black music soaring!
    They jammed a stopper
by killing Holly,
    Valens and Bopper.

But the movement spun
    beyond control—
the Beatles grabbed
    America's soul.

They were out of reach
    of the Corporate venom
(though they got revenge
    by killing Lennon).

But by then the "damage"
    had all been done—
the walls were down,
    humanity won.

Art had rocked
    a mighty state
and rolled right over
    apart-hate.

501

"Before that happened,
    Gershwin, too,
had dared defy
    the Race taboo.

"His opus met
    a wall of hate,
and Gershwin died
    at thirty-eight."

502

Damage control
(or, Give us a break)
(by Uncle Sam)

In order to smokescreen
    the whole backfired thing,
they hype up the image
    of the—ah—"king".

503

"When you check the score
    on what Art can do
when artists have guts,
is it any wonder

"Bob Dylan's Rolling
    Thunder Review
beat Operation
Rolling Thunder?"

Tribute to the Vietnamese
(by Uncle Sam)

This people tops
    the Hebrew king;
at least *that* David
    had a sling.

Rockpont! Hairy man!
(by Uncle Sam)

What are we really
    accomplishing here?
Crossing the last
    taboo frontier.

We can finally mention,
    I assume,
the elephant in
    the living room.

"They're only mortal,
    yet they choose to fill
the Earth with horror—
    torture, kill—

"It's been like that
    since the world began,
the pivotal mystery
    of man."

507

"Hey, you aspiring
    Macdonalds and Bryans,
do they teach you all this
    in Political Science?

"We know you can't winkle it
    out of the media,
but why not from any
    encyclopedia?

"There are many neat things
    to be learned at U,
but nothing that threatens
    you-know-who."

508

Uncle Sam says,
    "It's nothing but vexity,
hacking your way
    through written complexity.

"Writers should leave you
    all smiley and dimply;
anything *worth* saying
    can be said simply."

509

"Authors should tote
    in their bag of tricks
a little shortening
    for their mix.

"It's not applicable
    to your rhymes,
but I feel I'm sentenced to death
    at times."

510

Novel approach
(by Uncle Sam)

I won't read 600 pages—
    sorry;
two hundred? Well,
    that's a different story.

511

"In writing, less
    means lesser sin;
what's left out validates
    what's in."

512

"It sometimes takes effort
    ad infinitum
to create an effortless
    little item."

513

"*. . . and sometimes not*"

"Six little words,
    but they'll live on and on:
'Can't we all
    just get along?'"

Fun question
(by Uncle Sam)

Humor: literature
    discloses
lots of it
    in Homer, Moses.

Aristophanes
    made cracks,
Plautus too,
    and sundry hacks.

But they told no jokes—
    not jokes per se,
like Shakespeare, Swift,
    or Rabelais.

So the question arises:
    exactly when
did the first real joke
    leave the author's pen?

Who was the first
    to cheer or jeer
his fellow man
    with "Did you hear . . . "?

This was a dude
    as great and real
as the inventor
    of the wheel.

It *would* be nice,
    when troubles splat you,
to pause a moment
    at his statue.

515

Though my Uncle Sam
    didn't ever marry,
he's lived for years
    with his girlfriend Sherri.

I don't quite get it,
    but that's their state;
he calls her his
    approxi-mate.

516

My Auntie Sherri,
    who teaches school,
said, "I try to live
    by the Golden Rule;

"But when you're threatened
    with gun or shiv,
the goldenest rule
    is the will to live."

517

Auntie Sherri
    was reminiscing
'bout the recent past
    she was sadly missing.

"The tides of change
    will inundate us;
the status quo
    has lost its status."

518

Aunt Sherri was watching
a Thirties flick:
"In those days they knew
how to make it click.

"They understood
the human heart;
how the sorrows of life
are the joys of art."

519

"They call them 'movies',
for obvious reasons,
and they moved emotions
in other seasons.

"No longer those feeling
communicators,
they do move me rapidly
out of theaters."

520

"Movie making
is quite a skill—
they have technological
overkill.

"But they have no map
or nomenclature
for points of convergence
in human nature.

"Though they hold the mirror up,
that glass
shows nothing but themselves,
alas."

521

"Producers, directors,
    in mental diapers—
a generation, perhaps,
    of hypers?"

522

"'One touch of nature
    makes the whole world kin'—
these infants wouldn't
    know where to begin—
so they cover with something they *do* know—
    din."

523

Playing the Audience
(by Aunt Sherri)

Tugs at its heartstrings
    is what it deserves—
since they can't furnish that,
    they grate on its nerves.

524

"Here's a stricture
    short and lucid:
Portraying emotion
    doesn't *produce* it."

525

"Two hours in dragsville—
    bring your pillows;
ever hear
    of subplots, fellows?

526

"It's simple really—
    if you're gripped,
look no further
    than the script.

"But when the film
    is in the can,
the writer is
    an also-ran.

"Yet writers can't
    complain of slighting,
since suffering
    improves their writing."

527

Less is More
(by Aunt Sherri)

The greatest of Special Effects
    you find
in the Theater
    of the Mind.

528

Aunt Sherri said, "We were born to trouble
    (as Job bemoans) as the sparks fly upward;
we try to abstain from the cup of sorrow,
    but fate keeps pressing our poor lips cupward.

"My love is agony, but no way
    am I prepared to see the back of it;
love is a constantly gnawing pain,
    but so, as the whole world knows, is the
        lack of it."

529

"Is there such a thing
    as this 'love / hate'?
you bet your bippie—
    try me and my mate.

"We love them—
    nothing can divert us;
but we hate them
    for their power to hurt us."

530

"He's a difficult guy
    with whom to jibe—
he's a member of
    the dia-tribe."

531

"It's a hell of a note
    and it hurts through and through
when your port in the storm
    is the storm itself too."

532

"The highway of life
    is no fun to hie on
unless it accords us
    a shoulder to cry on."

Famous Pairs
(by Aunt Sherri)

Simon and Garfunkel
   rented a stadium,
but Simon and Schuster
   booked the Palladium.
Costello and Abbott
   suffered daily
playing bit parts
   for Barnum and Bailey,
while Laurel and Hardy
(moral but tardy)
rejected a show
by Lerner and Loewe.
Ginger Rogers and Fred Astaire:
there was a razzle-dazzle pair!
They would have been able to steal a scene
from even Napoleon and Josephine.
Wolfe and Montcalm
each recited a psalm
before they died;
Jekyll and Hyde
were one and the same
except in name;
(and not related,
   as far as one knows,
to Heckle and Jeckle,
   those nattering crows).
Gilbert and Sullivan,
   you'll agree,
were as totally different
   as could be,
but two who travel
   the same fast track
are the irrepressible
   Frick and Frack.

Rolls and Royce
      made lots of deals,
and wound up being
      two big wheels;
but the biggest wheels
      we've seen in years
are Mickey and Minnie
      Mouse's ears.
Edgar Bergen
      and Charlie McCart'y
each owed much
      to the other party,
while Black and Decker
      got their start
by drilling the cast
      for Rodgers and Hart.
David and Goliath,
      strong and daring,
Samson / Delilah,
      what a pairing!
The relationship
      of Cain and Abel
in brotherly terms
      was a bit unstable,
and gave tremendous
      cause for grief
to their aging parents,
      Adam and Efe.
(So heed your conscience,
      it's just the ticket;
remember Pinocchio's
      Jiminy Cricket.)
Now Scarlett and Rhett
should never have met,
while Lois Lane
      and Superman
became each other's
      biggest fan.

Still, some folks favor
   Batman and Robin,
Earth-born dudes
   who ran the whole mob in.
Tarzan and Jane,
   brave and supple:
there's the original
   swinging couple.
Sweet Li'l Abner
   and Daisy Mae
topped the comics
   in their day;
then the prize
   for being loopy
passed to Charlie Brown
   and Snoopy.
Mutt and Jeff
   were short and tall,
but which was which
   I can't recall;
it's not the same
   with Jiggs and Maggie:
she was tall,
   he, short and saggy.
Jonah and the whale
had a tale and a tail,
while Captain Ahab—
   a trifle sick—
met his match
   in Moby Dick.
The wolf is known
   as a people-eater
through pairings with Riding Hood
   and Peter:
but the truth of the matter is,
   wolves esteem us;
just ask Romulus
   and Remus.

And here's an odd duo:
a boy and a green stalk;
who could this be except
Jack and his Beanstalk?
Now for a classy,
glassy gripper:
Cinderella's
wayward slipper.
William Tell
had dash and flair,
and with his apple
makes a pair.
A puppet show
by Punch and Judy
tells the tale
of Sleeping Beauty:
now the Prince
is in the wings,
and gets his chance
by pulling strings.
Robin Hood
and Friar Tuck
had more scrapes
than Tom and Huck,
and the things they knew
about how to hide
would have added years
to Bonnie and Clyde.
Frankenstein's monster
and Frankenstein
were desperate for
a place to dine,
so Hansel and Gretel
saw they were fed
by presenting a feast
of gingerbread.
(They accepted no payment,
fat or slim;

it was on the house—
      check the Brothers Grimm.)
Good King Arthur
      and his Table Round
fought wrongdoing
      to the ground,
and Lancelot
      and Guinevere
celebrated
      with a beer.
Romeo and Juliet—
      their saga still trots on,
as do the doings
      of Holmes and Watson.
And don't your spirits
      rise like yeast
at the story of Beauty
      and her Beast?
Anthony
      and Cleopatra
imported syrups
      from Sumatra,
while the Lone Ranger
      and his faithful Tonto
bought their stirrups
      in Toronto.
Can you add some more to these famous
      pairs?
Then you might try trios (you could start
      with bears).

534

Bear with me
(by Aunt Sherri)

Most kids should be happy
      with three bears—BUT—more bears
are always at hand, since
      we all have our forebears.

My Grandpa says,
    "There's no remission
from what someone called
    the human condition.

"You can't help feeling
    the way you do,
but it helps to know others
    feel that way too."

My Grandpa says,
    "When your grandma died
all the package
    came untied.

"All of a sudden,
    in a flash,
all priorities
    turned to ash.

"What's important
    we rarely know
until the day
    we see it go.

"One life's too little
    to get it right:
you need one life
    just to find the light;

"You're thrown in the ocean
    and can't swim a stroke;
it takes one life
    just to get the joke."

537

Love
(by Grandpa)

Before we die
    we've likely found
it's true, love makes
    the world go 'round.

The mother grouse
    who flops away
so her small treasures
    won't be prey;

The bear who gladly
    lets life go
to save her cubs
    from gun or bow;

The human parents'
    years of tears
to offer children
    good careers,

And always there
    as last resort
(there are no judges
    in love's court)—

Reflecting in
    our earthly station
the hidden love
    of the Creation:—

This isn't "love"
    of grope and leer,
but this is Love,
    Earth's atmosphere.

538

"Though declaration
    can be a token,
the greatest love
    remains unspoken."

539

"If there were no danger
    and death and despair,
how would we know
    that Love was there?"

540

Sad mortality
(by Grandpa)

A sad life drags
    like a floppy shoe;
a happy life flies,
    and that's sad too.

541

Grandpa reads Shakespeare
    and just adores him—
he's one writer
    who never bores him.
"He reveals human nature,
    appeals to our senses,
and gives no offence
    while tearing down fences."

"Shakespeare?" said Grandpa,
     "A man named Meres—
a total unknown
     for all these years.

"The secret lay bare
     to the 'merest' glances,
through well-known words
     by his offspring Francis.

"The Sonnets provided
     a simple key,
so the question is
     why none could see.

"For four hundred years
     we've believed some fellow
largely illiterate
     wrote Othello.

"Which serves to highlight
     the Bard's main theme:
knowledge can flow
     in a widening stream,

"But knowledge of Man—
     our secret core—
comes up against
     a steel-barred door.

"We can conquer space
     to the farthest stars,
but we'll never ever
     break those bars.

"Which is why most characters
        writers draw,
in six months time
        are dead as straw.

"But 'Shakespeare's' characters
        never dim;
that door was opened wide
        for him.

"A humbling thought!
        And that's the start
of brand-new wisdom
        and a brand-new heart."

Walk humbly with thy God
(by Grandpa)

When the man they call "Shakespeare"
    wrote *King Lear*,
was he giving his final
    testament here?

He portrayed human types
    you'd like to know,
some you wouldn't,
    and some so-so.

Pervading the play
    are a lot of those veteran
slurs at creatures
    we think we're better than.

(As well as allusions
    to cruelties
we inflict on breathers
    such as these.)

The play invites us
    to check our seeing:
is there special worth
    in the human being?

Well, even Cordelia
    should give us pause:
she'll slaughter thousands
    in *her* just cause.

And Edgar? In veiled
    disparagement,
he turns at the end
    on the loyal Kent.

Edgar and Edmund—
    hardly the same,
but linked, as humans,
    in more than name.

I look at myself
    and I know it's true:
we're an all-points mixture
    through and through.

Our master-race pride
    must be interred;
that seems to be "Shakespeare"'s
    final word.

544

"If you're wanting 'loyalty'
    defined,
what doggone species
    springs to mind?"

545

"*Man's work*"
(a quote from Lear *presented by Grandpa)*

Captain: I cannot draw a cart,
or eat wild oats. If it be man's work,
I'll do't.[*]

---

[*] "It" is a request to murder, for reward. And do't he does.

252

546

Uncle Delbert
    and Auntie Claire
have six kids
    to grin and bear.

He spoils them, but
    gets in his digs:
"They're just a bunch
    of gimme pigs."

547

Uncle Delbert
    is rich as Croesus
through building and renting
    on government leases.

"When you build for the state
    you can't go wrong;
recession, depression,
    it keeps going strong.

"If they had a Department
    For Getting Things Smaller,
the buildings it used
    would get taller and taller."

548

"An explanation
    for our plight:
the Left, it seems,
    is never right."

549

Uncle Delbert says
  he disagrees
with a lot of my verses'
  "radicalese".

"They sound like they're written
  by some pinko amateur;
what meter you using?
  Iambic pestameter?"

550

"I wouldn't invest
  a jot of my time
in your cornycopia
  of rhyme.

"Where's the demand for it?
  Who would fund it?
When did I ever
  need a pundit?

"But then, who knows?
  You might find some reader
whose wish is, 'Take me
  to your lieder.'"

551

"A standup comic
    gets tired and damp—
writers can sit with their wit
    and tramp.

"Someone should force them
    to stop and trim it;
you can't go joking
    without a limit.

"We've got liquor laws, sex laws,
    a parking *tag* law;
I think it's high time
    that we had a *gag* law."

"If that's a too
      ambitious goal,
we could start out
      with pun control.

"We'd offer cash
      and gifts in tons
to folks surrendering
      their puns,

"According them
      a certain date
beyond which time
      we'd confiscate.

"Those who could prove
      they're just collectors
need never fear
      the pun inspectors.

"But wait—that can't,
      by rights, excuse them—
if puns are there
      someone might use them.

"The ban, I think,
      should be complete
to get those zappers
      off the street."

"We're big on garbage
　　getting small;
one bag a week,"
　　said I, "is all."

But Uncle Delbert
　　gave me a look:
"When it comes to garbage
　　you wrote the book."

Then he asked me what
　　in the world I've been smoking,
but wound up saying
　　he was only joking,—

'Cause Auntie Claire
　　had come along,
and she thinks that I
　　can do no wrong.

When barbs are thick
　　and praise is scanty,
everyone needs
　　that kind of auntie.

554

Cheers

We know there's stimulants
　　to avoid,
and if we don't
　　we'll be destroyed.

But there's one that's harmless
　　and doesn't fade:
a nice cool drink
　　of Accolade.

Crock and crack

We think of our times
    as a science-enthroned age,
but we're bombing ourselves
    right back to the stoned age.

Small victories
(by Uncle Sid)

I attended a talk
    on the evils of drinking;
we were lectured and hectored
    on living and thinking.

Then I entered a tavern
    and ordered a tall one—
I've a mind of my own,
    albeit a small one.

"The 'war on drugs'
    is falling flat;
'More cops!' they cry—
    I'll drink to that."

558

It helped anyway
(by Uncle Sid)

A string of disasters
    was so dismaying
that (quite unlike me)
    I took to praying.

But the lines were out
    (I am not jesting)—
All I got was
    "testing, testing".

559

Aunt Lil went to Cancun,
    she said she'd try it
to get some needed
    peace and quiet.
She returned complaining,
    "Some folks on vacation
live lives of noisy
    desperation."

560

Auntie Lil remarked,
    "When I host a 'do',
it never turns out
    like I wanted it to;

"There's so many boors
    around these days,
and they get on my nerves
    in so many ways,—

"I feel I want everyone
    ejected—
pleasant company
    excepted."

561

Aunt Lil called Mom,
    inviting her
to visit this
    astrologer.
Mom went, but said
    "Once is enough;
we Virgos don't
    believe that stuff."

562

Aunt Lil dropped in
    at her psychic's haunts,
but her psychic wouldn't
    address her wants.

He said he was booked
    till 6:15;
he said that her visit
    was unforeseen.

Auntie Lil says,
   "Since Ben passed on,
a lot of the joy of life
   has gone.

"Though I'm grateful for life,
   I feel less like pursuing it;
I feel I'm not living life,
   but doing it."

News Junkie

I got News,
you got News,
all God's children got NEWS!
We got it in our eardrums,
   we got it in our jaws,
popping in our eyeballs
   and sticking in our craws;
News! News! We all got News!
All God's children got News!

When we get to Heaven
   some fine day,
things will be peaceful,
   so they say.
None of that gun-crazed
   macho zeal,
gut-churning News
   with every meal—
Will I enjoy it?
   Hey, get real!
I'll feel I've been rooked
'cause they've got me hooked
on News! News! News!

565

I'm a guillty fan
    of the daily papers,
where I can inhale
    the latest capers.

They're filled with conflict
    of every kind:
the lode of horror
    is deeply mined.

There's surely some truth
    in their depiction,
but the total truth
    is greater than friction.

566

Down at the mall

Down at the mall there's fun and action,
enough to put you into traction,
down at the mall.
There's just no end to what we're buying,
or maybe only wishing, sighing,
or *say* we bought (we could be lying)
down at the mall.

But still, it is a bit unnerving,
'cause we're *supposed* to be conserving,
and thinking small.
Oh well, it's certainly a blast;
I don't know if it's going to last;
but while it does, let's all live fast
and have a ball
before the fall
down at the mall.

567

How many *things*
    does one man need?
Our GDP
    is gross indeed.

Refusing to
    retrench and shrink,
we could be malled to death
    I think.

568

It's a Wonderful Life

Every day
    brings a new rendition
on the theme, The Glories
    Of Competition.

It needs the hype,
    since Cooperation
is the obvious motor
    of civilization.

569

Keeping a cap on it

Produce, produce,
    compete, compete,
and our poor planet
    takes the heat.

We're just its guests, though,
    we don't rule it;
we'll be engulfed
    unless we cool it.

570

The Cold War's over,
    can't you tell?
The world is warming up
    real well.

The iron curtain's gone,
    that's certain,
but we'll never lack
    for an irony curtain.

571

Conducting business
    for the good of all—
that thought drives Wall Street
    up the wall.

572

Things will go even better

There's still some spaces
    largely free
of advertising's
    mockery.

But this is bound
    to change, and soon—
the Corporations
    want the moon.

573

Markets are fine
    and so is "more",
but the bottom line
    is the ocean floor.

574

True, life is growth,
    and now the tack
is forging growth
    in cutting back.

575

We're Earth's compassionate stewards—
    NOT!
Who could have guessed
    what man hath rot?

576

We've turned the oceans
    into "seas of slaughter",
but we *do* pour oil
    on the troubled water.

577

Walls of Death

Ecclesiastes—
    who can forget
his imprecation:
    "evil net".

And now the net
    has spread by stealth
and snarled the planet
    in its filth.

578

I'd love to pay tribute,
    if I were a poet,
to Captain Paul Watson
    and Farley Mowat.

There's many more
    I'd be proud to honor,
for example, singer
    Sinead O'Connor.

Since I can't mention all,
    let these three stand
for Earth's conservers,
    scorned and banned.

579

As Spaceship Earth
    pops rivets, we
have cause to doubt
    its destiny.

Yet Spaceship Earth
    takes off and lands
without our say.—
    It's in good hands.

580

Every atom in its appointed place

Nature seems wild, unplanned, unkempt,
    while in the works of Man are found
(we think) precision, order—but
    it's just the other way around.

If any fault's discernible
    in Nature (to my tiny mind)
it's just it's taking so damn long
    (in human terms) to tame mankind.

581

Blood and race,
    class, clan and caste—
Spaceship Earth cries out,
    Avast!

582

Prescription for
the final war:
Match a sorehead
with a warhead.

583

Breathes there the man with soul so dead
    (or woman—there's no need to "man" it)
who never to himself has said
    "This is my own, my native planet"?

584

To ease our planetary
    stress,
takes planetary
    consciousness.

An apposite
    effect's in play:
the nation notion
    fades away.

But I think we'd mostly
    be appalled
to find this street we travel
    walled.

585

"Globalization"
    shouldn't be
just a plum
    in a family tree.

586

Market farces

Global markets
    applied to food
destroy, denature,
    and denude.

When Wall Street has
    the world in tow,
impoverished
    is what we'll grow.

'Free trade' frolics

Smallpoxed blankets,
    opium wars,
once knocked down
    resistant doors.

Subtler methods
    now prevail—
at least until
    they're seen to fail.

Crafty advertising
    gets
cash-from-death
    through cigarettes,

Baby formula
    and so.
Everybody's
    happy, no?

Lots in a name

The Nazi "New Order"
        went to hell,
but much of its spirit's
        alive and well.

We've a sacred trust
        to guard our border
against this Wall Street
        "New World Order".

Atlas Shrugged
*(first-ever interview elicits less-than-
enthusiastic comment)*

"When I took a look
        at this 'new world'
I must confess
        I almost hurled."

These "waves of the future"
        we've seen before;
they're responded to best
        with a wave from shore.

591

Wall Street Serenade

"Will you come into my parlor?"
    said the spider to the fly;
"You really can't avoid it
    for my parlor is the sky

"And everything beneath it—
    but my stewardship is noble;
you'll prosper when your destiny
    is gobble—I mean global."

592

Canada's a smorgasbord
    of anglophones and francophones,
the rest are titled "allophones",
    the integrators "yankophones".
The telephone itself was born
    in Canada, one hears,
so guess it's fitting we've got "phones"
    coming out our ears.

593

We once envisioned
    Ottawa
the focus of
    our Shangri-la.

A bit too rich
    for our lords' persona;
their speed is Tombstone,
    Arizona.

594

Showdown at the latrines

When their Wall Street masters
    hand them mop and pail,
just hear them bellow
    the OK Chorale.

And they do a good job
    cleaning those joints;
they're eager to earn
    their brownie points.

595

"Bordering on Aggression"

Panama
    (3,000 dead),
poor Granada,
    stomped and bled—

They're close to "Canada"
    phonics-wise,
and Fort Drum's close
    as the bullet flies.

596

"Banana republics"
    we parrot—thus
showing how Bro
    has brainwashed us.

We try to flatter Bro,
    not restrict him,
and blame their sorrows
    on the victim.

597

Get the whole world
　　singing your tune,
importing your "culture"
　　of rock and roon—

While you hook them onto
　　your life machines—
hey, no need
　　to dispatch Marines.

598

Tombstone culture
(a hundred million handguns)

You can be rolling in dough,
　　but material bounty
seems a marginal perk
　　when you're dead in Dade County.

599

The culture is loud,
　　but some demur—
the ones who use
　　a silencer.

600

One thing you can say—
　　if you don't mind puns—
re the U.S.A.:
　　it sticks to its guns.

601

We're swamped by images
        that we see
on largely American
        TV.

When you're treated as just
        a colonized rube,
your identity
        goes down the tube.

602

You know your country's
        ticker ticks
when you're able to see
        your very own flicks.

When another country
        controls your screens,
you're just a bunch
        of human beans.

Maple Disbelief

Attending a game
    at Carlton and Church
almost shocked me
    out of my perch.

Leering through
    that storied ice
was a huge Coca-Cola
    logo—twice.

Believe it—they huckstered
    the caffeined goo
where it interfered
    with the actual view,—

A literal case
    of having to yield
the ownership
    of our playing field.

But perhaps I shouldn't
    be crying shame—
it is (or *was*)
    only a game.

The blueprint for
the "new" (sic) world
of "après moi . . . "
    is showing plain;
the Corporations
talk "free trade",
by which they really
    mean "free rein".

Big-Time Grotesque
(FTA / NAFTA—"a monstrous swindle":
Trudeau)

Smashing jobs and lives
    as they make their grab,
they croon that everything's
    simply fab—
it's like Bluebeard rising
    from the slab
while Nero fiddles
    the Danse Macabre.

606

Massah say, Drop dead

It's funny—just
    as we bring our nation
to the brink of actual
    civilization—

A prototype
    in all its variety
of a necessary
    world society—

With brains and heart
    and rich resources
to mitigate
    the market forces—

We're told this nation's
    obsolete—
though huge, too small—
    it can't compete—

So we let the world's
    best hope, just go—
we don't want to make
    a fuss, you know.

607

Our role, they'll have it
    understood,
is drawing water,
    hewing wood.

We thus can be
    a useful pawn
until the wood
    and water's gone.

608

Fatal Fatalism

"It could be worse"—
    that's nicely reflective,
and show's a person's
    got perspective.

But the best perspective
    when you're in a pit
is looking for ways
    to get out of it.

609

True North, weak and free for the taking

Canucks are told
    to profess devotion
to a monarchy
    across the ocean.

And a portion do,
    though Ottawa
would be enough for most,
    n'est-ce pas?

If we feel that way,
    our rulers deride us;
they love those symbols
    that divide us.

610

Smile! You're a Star!
(in the Stars and Stripes)

If you love your country
    and want to abet it
by "nationalistic" stuff,
    forget it.

Our ruling class
    is wimpy and puppety—
they're warned not to let
    the peons get uppity.

611

Ask John Gray

Pro-Canada songs
    just won't score air time;
the Compradors
    are warned: don't share time.

Their slogan (practiced
    to the hilt):
"Let a hundred
    flowers wilt."

612

Putting out fires
    in trashed Kuwait
was one of those feats
    that make us great.

In a few short months
    we completed a job
scheduled for years.
    Did your heartstrings throb?

Not likely; our media
    kept the story
carefully screened
    from its repertory.

The Great White North
    must shut its mouth;
glory is handled
    from the South.

613

But bring back Broadfoot

Well, Canada, tidings
    of joy are sparse,
but one you have
    is ye olde Air Farce.

As Manifest Destiny
    hones its beak,
may the Farce be with you
    twice a week.

614

400 years of resistance

Another presence
    lighting our tortured
consciousness
    is David Orchard.

The Fight for Canada
    tells it all—
how we learned to walk
    and *then* to crawl.

615

Brainwashed at School
(the Ginn effect)

Are we already
    a conquered land?
Our fabulous history
    is banned.

"Well-educated"
    people plow
through Orchard's book
    exclaiming, "Wow!"

616

Courageous pages

What Uncle Sam
    Really Wants—
Chomsky's exposé
    chills and haunts.

To be informed
    is to abhor
the sly veiled evil
    crouched next door.

Shining Knight needs Slavering Monster
(or, The Noriega Tango)

With the Cold War over
　　it's hard to fake it;
Wall Street's left standing there
　　gross and naked.

There's lots of "villains"
　　with whom to bait us—
who's the next to get
　　starring status?

There is a God

Every time
　　I'm feeling blue
I say "two seats"
　　and I'm good as new.

Canada's cold,
　　and the people have *felt* down,
but they're bound to be warmed
　　by the Tory meltdown.

A historic defeat,
　　a smashing rout—
could it be too soon
　　to count us out?

Charlatan Accord

A battle in the war
  for Canada's soul
was resolved at La Maison
  de l'Egg Roll.

The continentalists
  set their sights
on carving the land
  into easy bites.

With Wall Street Bro
  and his Ottawa grinch
directing things
  it seemed a cinch.

Their polls were soaring,
  no prob—but lo!
At the crucial moment
  appears Trudeau!

It was in the bag,
  could one man spoil it?
Yup—their vote
  went down the toilet.

We can still resist
  and fulfill our dream—
the individual
  reigns supreme.

Stand up, Canada

Cuba and Canada
　　fit real neat;
we should take their fruit
　　and send our wheat.

And in the winter,
　　when you want some sun,
head for Cuba
　　and jump the gun.

Cuba's crime
　　is written clearly:
the people value
　　life too dearly.

A fact of life
　　we often see:
life is cheap
　　when it isn't free.

The opposite
　　is just as clear:
when life is free
　　it's also dear.

A lesson abstracted
　　from humankind's wrangling:
treat others as puppets
　　and *you'll* be left dangling.

625

We saw a crash
    on 401
when an 18-wheeler
    slid and spun.

"Time is money",
    and so the roads
are suffocated
    with roaring loads—

Despite the fact—
    a small detail—
this cargo could be
    shipped by rail,

Or if not, sent
    in trucks that cede
control to governors
    of speed.

But that would mean
    a moral leap;
in North America
    life is cheap.

A *Just Society?*

If I've caught my Uncle
    Sam's neurosis,
it's from reading 'bout things
    like silicosis—

How thousands of miners
    are crucified,
their widows cheated
    on how they died,

And the murderers honored,
    their lives full of glamor,
while some poor lost pauper
    gets tossed in the slammer.

627

627

A *Just Society*

Go down, Moses,
let the people see
what you really meant
by your Jubilee.

Wealth always winds up
with a few—
the results are always
tragic too.

And as water always
seeks its level,
folks won't starve
while others revel.

Somehow the wealth
must be evened out—
as the soil's prepared
for the seeds to sprout.

It doesn't matter
how it's brought to be,
everyone must have
their Jubilee.

628

I'm pretty pragmatic
most of the time;
I'm not toeing any
particular line.

I *do* take up causes,
sometimes by the dozen,
but I know that an ism
can soon be a wasm.

629

A party line
    will drag you low;
it's such a heavy
    line to tow.

630

Flexibility's
    joyful, virile;
a dogma-eat-dogma world
    is sterile.

631

The sun isn't up
    to a very long visit
when it's raining cults and dogmas,
    is it.

632

Our century tells us
    nothing's unthinkable;
Titanic's the metaphor:
    "unsinkable".

633

Easy to say . . .

Remember the past
    so it won't be repeated—
but don't remember it
    more than needed.

634

Though feuds are difficult
    to smother,
must we bury the hatchet
    in each other?

635

Four-letter words—
    I know a gem
that explains our every failure:
    "them".

636

Let be
(by Grandpa)

A man who otherwise
    malingers
may be dynamic
    pointing fingers.

To point our finger back's
    not wise;
it's how he gets
    his exorcise.

637

"We're taking History
    by the throat
and mastering it",
    fanatics gloat.

But a Voice responds,
    "More modesty;
this is *my* story,
    as you'll see."

638

Epitaph for
　　fanatic myopia:
"A funny thing happened
　　on the way to Utopia."

639

On human gods

Progress lies
　　in coal and quarks;
Environment?
　　It's not in Marx.

640

Red for passion
　　I don't demean,
and words can be silver and gold,
　　I ween,
but life has a more
　　compelling sheen—
the colors of living,
　　blue and green.

641

Herstory
(by Grandpa)

The picture's there
　　to be revealed;
it's huge, complex,
　　and well concealed.

Each generation
　　helps a lot,
connecting up
　　another dot.

Name Game

The role of People's
    Advocator
reached its peak
    when it found its Nader.

It's strange how names
    suggest a tale—
remember Hooker's
    Love Canal?

The place where all
    that nuclear stuff
fell down to earth
    was what? Mars Bluff.

The ship that sank
    in quiet seas
was called *Titanic*
    if you please.

And the one that greed
    helped to capsize,
the *Herald of*
    Free Enterprise.

Lincoln was Kennedy's
    secretary,
and Kennedy Lincoln's.
    (This gets scary—

Connecting the two
    over the years
resonates
    with our deepest fears.)

And speaking of Abe,
    there's Abe Zapruder,
history's ultimate
    zap intruder.

In on the plot
    and trying to nip it
by spilling the beans
    was Officer Tippit?

Soviet power
    peaked at Yalta
and signed itself away
    at Malta.

The British Empire's
    birth and death
was framed by queens
    Elizabeth.

And though I don't
    condone such digs,
there's nudges re
    the Bay of Pigs.

And when we come
    to Viet Nam,
Westmoreland led
    for Uncle Sam,

While lying low
    and forced to hunker
in doomed Saigon
    was Ellsworth Bunker.

So what's it mean?
    Who knows? It's just
ironic glitter
    in the dust.

643

As my Grandpa views
    the world around,
this is what
    he says he's found:

"No amount
    of psychoanalysis
cures spiritual
    paralysis.

"Here are words
    I heard someone
mumbling in
    the midday sun:

"'Adler's addled,
    Freud's a fraud,
Jung's unstrung:
    it's back to God.'

"Seems a trifle
    too onesided,
but perhaps
    not all misguided.

"All of us
    should seek salvation
in deeper caring
    for Creation.

"But the winds of travail
    will still be blowing,
since life's designed
    to keep us growing."

644

A Jungian analyst
    lost his grip,
and grabbed his client
    by the hip;
it was, he blushed,
    a Freudian slip.

645

Jung and Freud
    both strove to know—
without offending
    the status quo.

They were hostage to
    unconscious (?) fears
of jeopardizing
    their careers.

646

Touchstone
(by Grandpa)

Psychiatry
    is somewhat sad;
it should be humble
    just a tad,
and realize
    each current fad
is subject to—
    is this so bad?—
the definition
    'Shakespeare' had:
true madness knowledge
    spurns the grad,
and rests with those
    who have been mad.

647

"Here's some truth
          without a stitch on:
things exist
          through opposition."

Grandpa points
          to the setting sun,
and says, "You know
          when day is done

"Because of the
          encroaching night;
without the dark,
          could we know light?

"Light lives through dark,
          and pain must be
if we're to taste
          felicity.

"Everything
          that is, is dual;
Man's compassionate
          and cruel.

"Life itself,
          there's no denying,
is the other side
          of dying.

"But as life can atrophy
          or flourish,
can we not choose
          which sides to nourish?"

Far Out
(by Grandpa)

A Doctor of Divinity
knows all about Infinity;
    to get his degree
    he sat at the knee
of God the Creator—didn't he?

The young theologian Fiddle
    refused to accept his degree;
"It's enough", he said, "being born 'Fiddle'
    without being 'Fiddle, D.D.'"

"But what's in a name?" he reflected,
    "I'm handsome, devout and gregarious;
I'll strive so that when they hear 'Fiddle'
    they'll instantly think 'Stradivarius'."

Artistic advice
(by Grandpa)

The way to be
    an innovator
is imitating
    the Creator.

Her knowledge must be
    far from small,
and yet She hardly
    speaks at all.

651

"As I reflect
    upon my day,
not much I strove for
    came my way.

"Life is such—
    as the old song goes—
you get two thorns
    with every rose.

"But in time you learn
    to pay the rent
that life demands,
    and to be content.

"Is being content
    (this may sound sappy)
not to be happy,
    being happy?"

Small annoyances

My Grandpa says,
   "A small annoyance
is all it may take
   to spoil our joyance.

"But it normally stands for
   something bigger—
the small annoyance
   is just the trigger.

"So putting the small
   annoyance right
is hardly designed
   to ease our plight.

"When we cotton to that,
   after many a year,
the small annoyances
   disappear.

"Of course we could argue
   without intermission
the small annoyance's
   definition."

653

All by myself
(by Grandpa)

Note the little child's
    squeal of joy
when her probing hands
    find a hidden toy.

It isn't the same
    when it's out in plain view—
there isn't that sense
    of the powerful *you*.

I feel that same joy
    each time I discover
you really *can't* tell
    a book by its cover.

654

An ethical universe
(by Grandpa)

Is morality really
    deep, deep seeing
into universal
    laws of being?

The symmetry
    of push and shove
within a frame
    of boundless love?

How easily all's
    misunderstood!
A lightning flash
    revealed it: "Good".

Mosaic world
(by Grandpa)

"Ah Love! could you and I with Him conspire
To grasp this sorry scheme of things entire,
    Would we not shatter it to bits—and then
Remold it nearer to the heart's desire!"

A kindred thought, in less anarchic way,
Isaiah uttered, yearning for a day
    when lions would associate with lambs
companionably, not to prey but play.

Misunderstand the world, and so abuse it—
our ignorance at one time might excuse it,
    but now the light of Moses' revelation
pervades the world, as we're at risk to lose it.

The Question
(by Grandpa)

"See how the Fates their gifts allot,
For A is happy—B is not.
Yet B is worthy, I dare say,
Of more prosperity than A!"

Yet maybe A's felicity
is not what it appears to be,
while B's deservings, doubtless great,
may not approach the estimate.

But still, we know the plaint is true;
there's so much left on Earth to do.
We must have justice on this ball
for all—but what is meant by all?

The answer's there for all to see,
but what it is we don't agree.
But when we do, it's my suggestion
we'll feel less need to raise The Question.

No-nonsense dreamer
(dreams of failure)

The dreams with which
    some people tussle
are a complicated
    jigsaw puzzle,
inciting "experts"
    to dig and probe,
cajoling the psyche
    to shyly disrobe.

Not mine! My dreams
    are so straightforward,
at the very first knock
    they swagger doorward,
and cry, "We're here!
    One nudge will launch us
straight as an arrow
    from your subconscious."

It doesn't take much
    interpretation
when I find myself
    at a railway station,
and I missed the boat—
    I mean the train—
as I feel I've done
    again and again.

I run behind it,
    I holler and holler,
but it keeps getting smaller
    and smaller and smaller,
and another train hits me—
    I wake with a scream—
inexpressibly thankful
    it was only a dream.

Or I'll be in a room
      writing exams:
the lights go off—
      a steel door slams—
it's not a question
      whether I failed;
I did, and here I am,
      scorned and jailed.

And so it goes—
      my dreams surround me
with recurring scenes
      that torment and hound me.
Would that I couldn't
      figure them out!
But it's all too clear
      what they're all about.

Hell-bent for election
(a dream of success)

Some work by week
    and some by hour,
some like money,
    some like power,
some like sweet
    and some like sour—
it's all the same to me.

Some are quiet,
    some are fussin',
some are bikin',
    some are bussin',
it's six of one
    and half a dozen
of the other to me.

Diversity,
diversity,
it's what the world was made to be;
There's thirty million kinds of insects,
so let's have joy sects, guilt sects, sin sects,
feasting, fasting, yang and yin sects,
    it all looks good to me.
All your proclivities,
wholesome activities,
    deserve to be honored—and free.

So there you have it;
    next election
I'm inviting
    your inspection;
I'm the closest
    to perfection
you're ever likely to see.

There's no one broader
        in perspective,
more inclusive,
        less rejective,
nobler, kinder,
        more effective
than moderate modest me.

Diversity,
diversity,
it's what the world was made to be;
Come people all, the worker, farmer,
banker, broker, hermit, charmer,
come to my arms, lay down your armor,
        you all look good to me.
Diverse as we know we are,
let's up and show we are
        able, this once, to agree—
        on *ME* !

659

In most of life's
        frenetic scrimmage,
it's best to have
        a clear-cut image.

But engaged in political
        hocus-pocus,
it pays to be slightly
        out of focus.

660

Basic footwork
(by Uncle Sid)

Here's a formula
    to achieve success
that can be applied
    with little stress:

Put your best foot forward
    when starting out,
and keep the other one
    out of your mout'.

661

Easy does it
(by Uncle Sid)

Consider the ant
    and then get wise:
they toil all day,
    those tiny guys,
lugging scads
    of awkward freight
dozens of times
    their size and weight,
never complaining,
    never stepping
aside to rest
    from their frenzied schlepping—
yet despite this constant
    grunt and pant,
have you ever heard
    of a famous ant?[*]

---

[*] You may think me prejudiced,
    I grant,
 but you're wrong—I'm far from
    anti-ant.

662

I can't control
    the way I feel,
but try to keep
    an even keel.

Exhilaration
    at the summit
is sure to hesitate
    and plummet.

663

Fred says my life will be a hex
until I graduate in sex;
but I resist his jeering shove—
I want it all, both sex and love.
Let others get upset and frantic;
me, I'm remaining a romantic.

664

Besides, there's always
    the danger question;
a little too toxic
    for my digestion;
my neck's exposed—
    I'm not a turtle—
we're not immortal,
    immune or infertile.

I feel like a part
    of myself is missing—
the part that wants to be
    hugging and kissing.

I feel like I'm drowning
    in a hostile ocean,
and the ocean is *me*
    not sharing devotion.

The ocean of self
    is shallow but wide,
and you'll never make it
    to the other side.

Signing off

My Grandpa says,
    "You'll always know
when it's the proper
    time to go.

"To stay as an
    unwelcome guest
puts friendship to
    a cruel test.

"Proverbs preach
    in every tongue:
Depart in time,
    keep friendship young."

I feel my Grandpa
    can't be wrong;
it's time to close
    my book of song.

I've been your guest
    and you've been mine;
I've loved our concourse.

Jeremy Fine